MOTORIZED MAIL

James H. Bruns

Published by

700 E. State Street • Iola, WI 54990-0001
Telephone: 715/445-2214

Please call or write for our free catalog of automotive publications. Our toll-free number to place
an order or obtain a free catalog is 800-258-0929 or please use our regular business telephone
715-445-2214 for editorial commentand further information.

ISBN: 0-87341-485-3

Printed in the United States of America

CONTENTS

ABOUT THE ILLUSTRATIONS

While we strive to publish the highest quality photographs possible, some of the illustrations presented in this book are from vintage newspapers. Because of previous half-toning, they are of relatively poor quality. Despite this, in many cases they are the only views that are available for certain vehicles. For this reason we have elected to include them.

ACKNOWLEDGMENTS

You cannot create a pictorial history without pictures and the photographs in this book came from many sources. I am indebted to each contributor. Many of the individuals who furnished illustrations or information are current or retired postal employees, including Harold Barnes, Jacob Cheeks, Joseph Cohen, Megaera Ausman, Jane Kennedy, Paul Rosenak, Robert St. Francis and George Shifflet. Others who have helped with this project are Stu Abraham, John Weimer and Nancy Pope.

EVOLUTIONS

MOTORIZING URBAN MAIL

With 202,000 vehicles currently on the road, the United States Postal Service has the largest vehicular fleet in the world. These vehicles drive 847 million miles per year. That is a far cry from the way things were a little less than a century ago when the first fragile-looking motor car was tested by the Post Office Department in 1899.

This scrapbook of archival and contemporary photographs highlights as much as possible the evolution of the nation's motorized mail vehicles. Some steps in this evolutionary process are not included because no photographs of these "missing links" have been found. For example, it is known that Detroit successfully used three automobiles over the 1902 Christmas holiday to collect mail. This was a significant step forward for the Post Office Department because one of the vehicles completed a trip in 40 minutes that typically took a horse-drawn mail wagon two hours to complete. The postmaster of Detroit, F.B. Dickerson, was so excited by the results of this test that on December 29, 1902, he wrote to Post Office Department headquarters saying "The machines were given a very severe test, inasmuch as during the two days that they were in operation we had a very heavy snowstorm. The results of the trial of these three machines were simply surprising. They accomplished so much more than we anticipated they would." Dickerson asked for permission to conduct other tests, and was promptly advised by Second Assistant Postmaster General W.S. Shallenberger that "The Department is interested in learning all it can of these tests, and will be glad to have you report if such tests as are proposed are found to be successful."

Another "missing link" involves the Los Angeles post offices use of an "auto mail wagon" early in 1910. This makeshift vehicle was used to pick up mail from boxes in all parts of the city between 11 a.m. and 9 p.m. The vehicle accommodated four clerks who canceled and sorted mail en route. No photographs of this vehicle, or those used in Detroit, have thus far been found, if any were ever taken.

Contractors Were First

The earliest mail trucks were operated by private contractors who furnished vehicles under contract to the Post Office Department. Such contracts usually were for several years, often required the contractor to provide the driver, and typically called for at least two vehicles to be provided (one served as a backup). More often than not, the type of vehicle that was used was specified in the contract. That certainly was the case with the contract for Norfolk, Virginia, for the period from April 1, 1915, to March 31, 1918. The contractor holder, Howard S. Meyer, was to furnish "One (1) Maxwell automobile wagon, with one in reserve, without chauffeur, to be used eight (8) hours each weekday, and as many hours on Sunday, not exceeding eight (8) as may be necessary."

The first government-owned mail trucks were acquired in 1906 for use in Baltimore, Maryland. Other acquisitions followed sporadically, including five 1,500-pound "KisselKar" delivery wagons that were purchased by the Post Office Department in February 1913 for use in conjunction with Parcel Post Service in Washington, D.C. These 35-hp light-duty

Parcel Post was a phenomenal success. During roughly the first five days of service, over four million packages were mailed. Over 300 million packages were handled during the first six months of service; and the inauguration of "Collect-on-Delivery" and "Insurance Services" later in 1913, only added to the popularity of Parcel Post.

trucks, manufactured by the Kissel Motor Car Co. of Hartford, Wisconsin, were selected by postal service engineers after seeing them exhibited at the New York auto show. The engineers were not alone in their opinion of the Kissels. At that time one leading newspaper reported that at such car shows, "The Kissel was a firm favorite with visitors."

Such small purchases of government-owned trucks were commonplace until the Post Office Department's 1915 appropriation was passed. Under that appropriation Congress authorized the establishment of the postal service's own "Motor Vehicle Service." This enabled the Post Office Department to go on its second major buying spree (the first came with the establishment of Parcel Post). As a result of this the use of contractor versus government-owned vehicles shifted dramatically.

When it was created on July 1, 1916, the Motor Vehicle Service was assigned to the Office of the First Assistant Postmaster General. It remained there until September 1921 when the function was transferred to the Office of the Fourth Assistant Postmaster General in conjunction with the creation of the newly formed "Division of Vehicle Transportation." This was a short-lived name change. The following month, the title of the operation was again changed, this time to the "Division of Motor Vehicle Service." Along with the change in title came a change in oversight. The function was once again returned to the First Assistant. Nine years later this division was reassigned to the Fourth Assistant's office.

So Many Makes and Models

For much of its history the Post Office Department has not played favorites. It has used steam-, electric- and gasoline-powered vehicles, and in about the same proportions as they were used personally, and commercially. Electric vehicles, for example, were almost entirely confined to cities or to interurban service where distances were not great

In the hopes of winning a future contract with the postal service, Oldsmobile furnished four delivery wagons to the Detroit, Michigan, post office for use during the 1902 to 1905 Christmas seasons. These trucks were used to transport mail between postal stations around town. The foursome pictured here were used in 1905.

After having temporarily used Oldsmobiles for the four previous years, in 1906 the postmaster of Detroit, Michigan, got the Rapid Motor Vehicle Co. to provide four delivery wagons to handle Christmas mail. These Rapids were used from December 19 to December 26 to transport mail between Detroit's postal stations.

and the roads were good. And, early electrics were popular, particularly among postal officials. Of the estimated 4,000 motor vehicles in New York City in 1913, 1,500 were electrics. In Chicago, where there were 2,000 motor vehicles that year, 400 were electrics. A rough census in 1913 showed that there were almost 45,000 motor vehicles of one kind or another nationwide. Of these, nearly one-fourth were in the state of New York. However, by 1925 electric vehicles had fallen from grace.

When it first appeared in 1895 the editors of *Horseless Age* observed that there were, to their knowledge, 73 entrepreneurs dabbling with gasoline, steam or electric vehicles. Many of these had

started out making bicycles or wagons, and nearly all wanted nothing better than to receive a big postal contract for an armada of their vehicles. Local postmasters were the first to take advantage of this, and Detroit's postmaster was among the earliest to capitalize.

Oftentimes local postmasters played one car company against another and ended up getting something for nothing. In the hopes of winning a future contract with the postal service, Oldsmobile furnished the Detroit post office with four delivery wagons each year during the 1902 to 1905 Christmas seasons. These trucks were used to transport mail between postal stations around town. The following

A lineup of newly delivered Model L "Vim" Parcel Post trucks. (Photograph courtesy of the United States Postal Service)

Fitted with snow chains, this mail truck was used in Kansas City, Missouri, to help inaugurate Parcel Post. (Photograph courtesy of the United States Postal Service)

year the postmaster of Detroit went to the Rapid Motor Vehicle Co. to see what it could offer. Rapid ended up providing four delivery wagons from December 19 to December 26. The automakers realized what was going on but, because of what was at stake, they were all too willing to go along with providing Uncle Sam with such short-term freebies.

This was especially true in conjunction with the introduction of Parcel Post in 1913. This tendency was reported in an issue of the *Los Angeles Sunday Times* this way: "The motorizing of the Parcel Post in most parts of the country is a certainty, and there is accordingly a keen rivalry among truck builders for this business."

Besides the expectation that Parcel Post would be good for sales, it also was predicted to have a major impact upon truck technology. The December 7, 1912, issue of *Harper's Weekly* emphasized this belief when it observed that "This building of motor trucks for the parcel post is expected to have a far-reaching influence on the motor truck trade in general. Not only will it bring in a vast grist of new orders and provide much ready money, but it will extend factories and greatly increase experiment and designing."

In the minds of most manufacturers, the attractiveness of immediate sales outweighed any anticipated technological benefits. Typical of the early automakers, Willys-Overland Co. jumped at the chance to let the Post Office Department use its line of trucks. In 1914, the automaker advised postal officials that it was "prepared to offer a line to cover any and all requirements of the postal service, from a light delivery car of 800 pounds capacity to the six-ton Garford trucks." The carrot of potential sales was precisely why so many car companies allowed the postal service to try out their products at little or no cost.

While such opportunities provided the postal service with a good basis upon which to convert from horse-drawn to motorized vehicles, it also showed postal officials how vulnerable such companies were. Within a decade the number of automakers would arguably have been up to nearly 500, had it not been for the relatively high mortality rate. Over one-half went out of business almost as soon as they began. Many succumbed to the frequent downturns of the nation's tidal economy (ups and downs in the economy were far more cyclic than they are now). Upturns and downturns tended to follow three to four year ebbs and flows. In the 1900s, many of the less secure companies that weren't wiped out by the Panic of 1907 were done in by the one that followed three years later.

Entrepreneurs entering the field in subsequent years didn't fare much better, and the resulting drop-out rate meant that by 1925 there was a significant glut of what one historian calls "orphan cars." The postal service was affected by this dropout. Repairing these orphan vehicles became a real nightmare.

Swamped With Mail

The Post Office Department faced perhaps its first motor vehicle-related challenge in 1913 when Parcel Post was inaugurated on January 1. While this was briefly alluded to before, the Post Office was totally unprepared for the public's response to the new package service. In the first few days of service it was swamped with parcels building to a deluge of four million packages during the first week of service. Postmaster General Frank Hitchcock quickly realized what he was up against. He hastily issued a call for bids for 100 government-owned mail trucks to augment the meager number of rented trucks that were being furnished by contractors and the few government-owned mail trucks that were then in service—vehicles that he confessed were "already taxed to their utmost capacity."

The challenge was to select the best possible motor vehicles in the shortest time, but most manufacturers were so new that they did not have well-established track records for reliability and service. Also, the Post Office Department did not have well-defined specifications for what it wanted. This resulted in the creation of a hodgepodge fleet of conventional and unconventional delivery vehicles.

Some of the more unusual vehicles, such as the Decatur Motor Car Co.'s "Cyclecar" or the three-wheeled "Duryea Gem" are not depicted because of their limited use.

Local postmasters added to the mishmashed fleet, often opting to acquire vehicles made in their city or state. The problem with this was that many suppliers were not around a few years later. Most had gone out of business.

Almost as soon as these vehicles were acquired they began to be abused. To prevent this, a series of operating rules was established—with harsh penalties for drivers who ignored them. But the workload made adhering to such rules difficult. One of the most frequently broken was that of overloading the vehicles. Mail trucks were often loaded well beyond their capacity. Such overloading often resulted in the temporary loss of mailbags in transit. As a safeguard, a tarp was typically used to cover the mound of mailbags and a laborer often rode on top of the load so any that did manage to drop off could be promptly recovered. The tarp also protected the

A typical example of an overloaded postal vehicle. Mail handlers tended to never know when to stop piling on the mailbags.

mail from moisture. The problem of weighing down vehicles was not confined to the Post Office Department. The tendency to overload all types of commercial vehicles was common during much of the first quarter of this century.

No Substitutions in Sight

The next significant challenge arose during the Great Depression. The array of equipment then in use was comprised mainly of worn-out vehicles and money for new purchases was hard to come by. A few thousand three-quarter-ton and one-and-one-half-ton trucks were purchased between 1929 and 1931. Fifty percent of the smaller vehicles were Model A Fords. Seventy-five percent of the larger trucks were Model AA Fords. The remainder of the three-quarter-tonners were principally from Chevrolet (14 percent) and Hudson/

Essex (36 percent). In the one-and-one-half-ton size, Chevrolet furnished all of the remaining 25 percent. With the outbreak of World War II, these trucks had to be kept on the road until well after the war. By 1945, over 90 percent of the postal fleet was obsolete.

A Time For Change

The 1950s and 1960s was a time of great change. This period was marked by a greater reliance on contract carriers and the acquisition of a variety of "new" government-owned vehicles that were built to well-defined Post Office specifications.

Beginning in 1952, and for about a decade thereafter, the Post Office Department went on a major buying spree. This buying binge reflected the pent-up needs of a department that had been deprived of purchases of motor vehicles because of the Great De-

By the mid-1950s postal officials considered vehicles such as this 1949 International Harvester one-and-one-half-ton Model KB-5 to be overweight and cumbersome. They also hated the fact that it had double rear tires. As part of their long-range vehicle planning program that was designed to phase out all pre-1950s vehicles, postal officials opted to replace the KB-5s with Chevrolet forward control vans. Such vans afforded up to a third more capacity, weighed half as much, offered better visibility, were right-hand drive, and were easier to maneuver.

pression and World War II. The number of vehicles purchased and the array of styles was astounding.

The chart (see chart on following pages) identifies the array of vehicles purchased between 1952 and 1961.

The use of over-the-road contractors also grew dramatically between 1958 and 1968. Annual payments for highway mail transportation increased from $82.6 million to $185 million during that ten-year span. This growth was largely due to the loss of railway mail service throughout the country. The growth also reflected the tremendous increase in mail volumes and the creation of sectional mail processing centers that relied upon truckers to move the mail.

Many of the "new" vehicles tested in the 1950s and 1960s were experimental, including a number of three- and four-wheel "carrier carts." Some of these were so small that they were designated "very light vehicles." While these test models were among the earliest attempts to motorize letter carriers, these impractical contraptions fell far short of the hoped for success. Although the box-fronts on some models safely accommodated about 250 pounds of mail, none of these cabless carts protected the carriers from foul weather.

A Modern Approach

The most recent change in the way the Postal Service acquires vehicles resulted in the purchase of over 144,000 new "Long-Life Vehicles." These units were selected as a result of a competition that involved three different vehicles pitted against each other in a winner-take-all endurance contest. The 24,000-mile trial, which went on for 20 hours a day, seven days a week, for four months, has been characterized as the most grueling test of a government

The Grumman Allied test vehicle being put through its paces at the Texas test track. (Photograph courtesy of the United States Postal Service)

vehicle since the M-1 battle tank. The winning vehicle, supplied by Grumman Allied Industries, was subjected to 11,520 miles of gravel roads, 960 miles of cobblestones, and another 960 miles of potholes. It is estimated that the Grumman vehicle hit the same potholes 35,000 times. Half of the time the vehicle was loaded down with 1,000 pounds of sandbags to simulate mail, while the rest of the time the cargo bay was empty. The competition resulted in the selection of what the Postal Service expects to be the workhorse for the 21st century.

The Postal Fleet Today

The United States Postal Service currently maintains a fleet of 202,224 vehicles. The bulk of these vehicles provide transportation primarily for the postal system's carrier delivery network. In addition to its carrier-related vehicles, the Postal Service uses approximately 9,600 vehicles to haul mail between postal facilities, airports and major mailers' facilities. And, besides the 202,224 postally-owned vehicles, another 6,555 vehicles are leased by the Postal Service.

Of those vehicles that are owned by the Postal Service, the largest number are half-ton "Long Life Vehicles." The Postal Service has 144,934 of these half-ton vans.

The following additional vehicle types were in use in Fiscal 1996:

VEHICLE TYPE	NUMBER
One-quarter ton	27,231
One-ton	1,613
Two- and Two-and-one-half ton	6,502
Five-ton	35
Seven-ton	914
Tractors	1,757
Tractors, Spotter	406
Trailers	4,816
Plant maintenance vehicles	2,864
Vehicle maintenance service vehicles	1,528
Administrative vehicles	7,383
Mobile post offices	201
Miscellaneous vehicles	276

These efficient vehicles, operating over predominantly well-paved roads, collectively logged over 1.1 billion miles in Fiscal 1996. But good roads have not always been the norm.

P.O.D. SERIAL NUMBER	TON GROUP RATING	YEAR MODEL	MAKE	MODEL NUMBER	ENGINE H.P.	WHEEL BASE	SHIPPING WEIGHT	PURCHASE PRICE
3051-4850	1/2-Ton	1952	Dodge	B-3-B	97	108"	3425	$1330.27
4900-6899	1-Ton	1952	Dodge	B-3-D	103	116"	5220	1762.02
7000-9124	2-Ton	1952	Dodge	B-3-G	114	128"	7640	2469.82
9200-10059	1/2-Ton	1954	Dodge-RHD	C-1-B6	110	108"	3345	1546.50
10100-10499	3/4-300	1954	Dodge	C-1-D6	110	108"	4685	2281.97
10850-11329	1/2-Ton	1954	Dodge-RHD	C-1-B6	110	108"	3295	1520.00
50000-53749	1-Ton	1951	Dodge	B-2-D	103	116"	5220	1417.89
510001-510004	1/4-Ton	1955	Willys	CJ3	60	80"	2015	2156.16
530001-532000	3/4-140	1955	Dodge-RHD	C-3-C6	115	95"	3710	2069.48
540001-540375	3/4-300	1955	International	RM-122	108	115"	5160	2277.14
620001-62100	3/4-200	1956	Chevy	3442	140	104"	5840	2210.79
630001-	3/4-140	1956	Chevy-RHD	3602				3119.79
630034-	3/4-200	1956	Intl-RHD	RM-110	108	102"	3800	6153.93
630035-630834	3/4-140	1956	Dodge-RHD	C-3-C6	115	95"	3820	2069.48
640001-640575	3/4-300	1956	International	SM-122	108	115"	5060	2277.14
670001-670006	Trail-20	1956	Fruehauf	FD-CD522			7500	3600.00
710002-711501	1/4-Ton	1957	Cushman	780-26	7.5	68"	860	917.50
720001-720250	3/4-200	1957	Chevy	3442	140	104"	5840	2210.79
720251-720875	3/4-200	1957	Chevy-RHD	3602	140	104"	5220	2403.91
720876-721775	3/4-200	1957	Chevy	3442	140	104"	5860	2319.53
730001-730200	3/4-140	1957	Dodge-RHD	C-3-C6	115	95"	3820	2094.48
730201-730620	3/4-140	1957	Chevy-RHD	3602	140		4920	2291.92
740001-740143	3/4-300	1957	International	SM-122	108	115"	5060	2298.14
740144-740973	3/4-300	1957	Chevy	3442	140	104"	6120	2337.13
760001-760002	Tractor	1957	White	3022PLT		96 1/2"	10164	7626.19
760003-	Tractor	1957	White	3020PLT		97 1/2"	5744	6960.63
760004-760007	Tractor	1957	White	3000T	130	103"	8310	9213.11
770001-770002	Trail-20	1957	Fruehauf	FD522-S			7200	3600.00
770003-770023	Trail-20	1957	Fruehauf	FD-120-S-SP				3600.00
770024-770027	Trail-35	1957	Fruehauf	FD-VVRT5535			10500	7270.88
810001-811778	1/4-Ton	1958	Cushman	780-107	8	67"	920	791.50
811779-813400	1/4-Ton	1958	Eshelman	300	9	71 3/4"	895	777.76
813401-	1/4-Ton	1958	Eshelman					2000.00
813406-813415	1/4-Ton	1958	Westcoaster	625	12.9	76"	1080	1550.00
813416-813542	1/4-Ton	1958	Cushman	780-107	8	67"	920	791.50
820001-820594	1/2-Ton	1958	Ford	78-A	145	116"	3400	*1496.25

P.O.D. SERIAL NUMBER	TON GROUP RATING	YEAR MODEL	MAKE	MODEL NUMBER	ENGINE H.P.	WHEEL BASE	SHIPPING WEIGHT	PURCHASE PRICE
830001-841250	3/4-140	1958	Chevy-RHD	3602	145	101 5/8"	4640	2158.30
840001-841250	3/4-300	1958	Chevy	3442	145	104"	5230	2298.90
850001-	2 1/2-Ton	1958	International	HME-162		179"	7750	6153.93
850002-850251	2 1/2-Ton	1958	International	AM-162	154	263"	8347	3898.29
860001-860005	Tractor	1958	White	3000T		91 1/2"	9420	8257.18
860006-860071	Tractor	1858	International	CO-202	175	99"	8500	5714.21
860072-860075	Tractor	1958	White	3000-T	220	109"	6440	7390.32
870002-870071	Trail-20	1958	Kingham	120TSPC-20				2294.18
910001-910317	1/4-Ton	1959	Cushman	780-107	8	67"	920	791.50
910318-910368	1/4-Ton	1959	Eshelman	300	9	71 3/4"	895	777.76
920001-921500	1/2-Ton	1959	Ford	59E	145	118"	3400	1537.43
930001-931000	3/4-140	1959	Dodge-RHD	M6-D200	120	98"	4700	2124.00
931002-931030	3/4-140	1959	Intl.-RHD	AM-80	112	96"	2800	2013.96
940001-941500	3/4-300	1959	Dodge	M6-P300	120	104"	5340	2239.00
950001-950063	2 1/2-570	1959	International	AM-162	154	149 3/4"	7750	3898.29
960001-960050	Tractor	1959	International	CO202	175	99"	9420	5714.21
960051-	Tractor	1959	White	3000T	220	109"	8500	7390.32
960052-960080	Tractor	1959	International	CO202	175	99"	9420	6074.82
970001-970060	Trail-20	1959	Kingham	120TSPC20			6440	2294.18
970061-970090	Trail-20	1959	Kentucky	VCKF			6800	2432.72
970091-970096	Trail-35	1959	COPCO	T3593CSB			10380	7000.00
010001-	1/4-Ton	1958	Westcoaster	625M				
010002-012402	1/4-Ton	1960	Westcoaster	650	129	77"	1150	998.33
020001-023210	1/2-Ton	1960	Willys-RHD	FDJ-3A	72	80"	3000	1925.53
030001-030020	3/4-140	1960	International	AM-80	112	96"	2800	2045.00
040001-041200	3/4-300	1960	International	AM-122	112.5	115"	4000	2135.00
050001-051250	2-1/2-570	1960	Chevy	C6302	130	157"	8120	6362.61
060001-060040	Tractor	1960	International	CO-202	175	99"	9876	7558.73
060041-060050	Tractor	1960	White	3000T	215	109"	10500	3145.21
070001-070050	Trail-20	1960	Dorsey	DF-20			6950	3454.66
070051-070070	Trail-28	1960	Dorsey	DF-20			8450	3574.06
070071-070105	Trail-32	1960	Dorsey	DF-20			9200	3677.64
070106-070120	Trail-35	1960	Dorsey	DF-20			9700	
110001-110599	1/4-Ton	1961	Westcoaster	650	12.9	77"	1150	998.33
110600-112099	1/4-Ton	1961	Cushman					
112100-112399	1/4-Ton (elec.)	1961	"Hicycle" (converted to gasoline)					
120001-120800	1/2-110	1961	Willys-RHD	FDJ-3A	72	80"	3000	1925.53
120801-122815	1/2							

P.O.D. SERIAL NUMBER	TON GROUP RATING	YEAR MODEL	MAKE	MODEL NUMBER	ENGINE H.P.	WHEEL BASE	SHIPPING WEIGHT	PURCHASE PRICE
122816-122835	1/2-Ton	1961	Chevy	R-1205	82	95"		1963.65
140001-140300	3/4-Ton	1961	International					2135.00
140301-140800	3/4-300	1961	Dodge					2321.51
140801-141300	3/4-300	1961	Dodge					2337.12
160001-160050	Tractor	1961	International	CO-202	175	99"	9876	6256.50
170001-170010	Trail-35	1961						
170011-170090	Trail-20	1961						

MISC. VEHICLES WITH PREFIX (LETTER) TO SERIAL NUMBER

P.O.D. SERIAL NUMBER	TON GROUP RATING	YEAR MODEL	MAKE	MODEL NUMBER	ENGINE H.P.	WHEEL BASE	SHIPPING WEIGHT	PURCHASE PRICE
T61 -T100	Tractor	1952	International	L-195	144	133"	7900	4131.00
T101 -T115	Tractor	1953	International	R-185	144	133"	8100	3661.69
T124-133, 144-160	Tractor	1954	International	R-182	145	130"	7400	*4382.99
T116-123, 134-143	Tractor	1954	White	3020PLT	130	85 1/2"	8115	5856.00
T161-T200	Tractor	1954	White	3020PLT	130	85 1/2"	8115	5539.57
T201-T310	Tractor	1954	International	R-182	145	130"	7400	2958.62
V-414 - V453	Trail-28	1954	Great Dane	ESV			7700	2490.76
V-454 - V533	Trail-32	1954	Great Dane	ESV			8300	2560.58
V-534 - V633	Trail-35	1954	Great Dane	ESV			8700	2630.41
V1 - V90	Trail-20	1950	Dorsey	DFC-S16			6150	1931.63
V91 - V180	Trail-20	1951	Highway	SKD-3703			6150	2063.21
V181 - V300	Trail-22	1952	Gramm	Tra-Van			6200	2060.00
V301 - V345	Trail-22	1953	Dorsey	DFC-S-16			6300	2179.49
V354 - V360	Trail-28	1954	Fruehauf	528			7920	3653.62
V361, 364, 380, 384, 386-388, 390, 392, 394-398, 400, 402, 404-409	Trail-30	1954	Fruehauf	530			8210	*3734.38
V350 V353	Trail-33	1954	Fruehauf	533			8670	3750.00
V346-349, 365-379, 381-383, 385, 389, 391, 393, 399, 401, 403, 410-413	Trail-35	1954	Fruehauf	535			8960	*3810.20
SV3-SV42	1/2-Ton	1954	Ford	Courier	115	115 1/2"	3500	1327.55
S105-S254	1-Ton	1954	Dodge	C-1-D6	103	125 3/4"	3705	1281.89
CS-1-CS100	3/4-Ton	1959	Willys	FC-170	105	103"	4000	*3198.96
CS101-CS125	3/4-Ton	1961	Willys					

* Indicates Average Price Of Vehicle.

FROM GUMBO TO GOOD RURAL ROADS

Before the turn of the last century, even the slightest summer shower or winter snow could transform an unpaved byway into an impassable brown gumbo-like quagmire. Up until World War I, the nation's roadways were almost entirely comprised of gumbo-prone paths.

The transition from gumbo to good roads was largely due to the mail. One of the greatest benefits of mail service was the creation of better roads. This was particularly true of long distance overland contract mail routes and Rural Free Delivery, more so than for City Delivery Service.

Long since retired letter carriers have said that they could always tell where the city limits were because that was where the paved roads stopped and the muddy paths began. When asked how many mud holes he had along his route, one turn-of-the-century carrier replied, "Just one, it begins where I leave town, and ends when I reach the brick street returning ...."

Good roads were a prerequisite for rural mail delivery, but some didn't take this mandate seriously. Following the introduction of RFD in 1896, thousands of requests for new routes poured into the postal service. Many of these requests were rejected because of "unserviceable and inaccessible roads." Along with the rejection letters, local governments began getting the message. If they wanted mail service, they and their constituents would have to improve and extend existing roadways, but this was not a painless process, nor was it expeditious.

In the end, the conversion from gumbo to good roads took more than a century to truly start.

The vision of the nation tied together by adequate roads was as old as the republic itself, but illusion and reality are two different things. After the Revolution, the main north/south post road, a route that would become U.S. Route One, was considered one of the finest roads by the standards of the day, but contemporary accounts of travel conditions show that much of the length of this boulevard was deplorable. According to the February 19, 1797, issue of *The American Annual Register*, "The roads from Philadelphia to Baltimore exhibited for the greater part of the way an aspect of savage desolation. Chasms to the depth of six, eight or ten feet occur at numerous intervals. A stagecoach which left Philadelphia on the 5th day of February, 1796, consumed five days in going to Baltimore. The weather for the first four days was good. The roads are in a fearful condition. Coaches are overturned, passengers killed and the horses destroyed by overwork put upon them. In wintertime no stage could set out for two weeks."

With only slight modifications, this description might just as easily be applied to road conditions for many locations nationwide as much as a century later. That was the case with U.S. Route One between Baltimore and Washington, D.C. As late as 1910, this roadway was only partially complete. From Washington northward to Bladensburg, Maryland, was paved, but thereafter for about a quarter of a mile the boulevard was untouched. From that point until College Park, the roadway was well maintained. After College Park there was another gap due to the fact that bridges were not yet constructed. From Beltsville to Contee, a five-mile section, the roadbed was unfinished. From Contee to Elkridge the highway was in fine shape, but from there into Baltimore was about as bad as the section north of Bladensburg.

The Post Office Department insisted that roads be maintained in good condition before agreeing to provide Rural Free Delivery service. To gain the service, local communities worked together to improve roads through their own labor or finance.

U.S. Route One wasn't America's only main artery. For commercial and military reasons, the Natchez Trace became one of the nation's first Federal roadway projects, although it's difficult to really call it that. The Trace was declared a post road in the early 1800s so that the biweekly "Great Mail" could reach Natchez, and soldiers were dispatched to make the necessary improvements. But little was actually done to this otherwise primal trail, except to slash away the underbrush, fill some minor potholes and clear away a few tree stumps. The end result was that the tract was upgraded only slightly. In this respect, the Trace was a prime early example of the way vision and reality collided in the tangible sense, but there were intangible conflicts emerging, too.

John C. Calhoun was among those who early on cherished the vision of improved roads. "Let us then bind the republic together with a perfect system of roads," he declared in 1816, but the reality was that it wasn't as simple as merely issuing such a call to action, and, as a latter-day staunch advocate for states' rights, Calhoun knew it. As a nation we could not quite seem to get past an ominous state versus Federal impasse, and as a result, our nation's growth was significantly hindered because of it for almost a century.

The idea of having the Federal government assume major responsibility for building and maintaining roads was hotly debated during the first quarter of the 19th century. President James Monroe hated the thought. He believed that roads were

17

Postal officials monitored road conditions and local postmasters were directed to halt service until needed repairs were made.

a local concern. To Monroe's way of thinking it was primarily the duty of the states to provide good roads for their people. Any question of Federal involvement was an affront to states' rights. This sentiment prevailed for much of the next century.

The states traditionally acknowledged that road building and maintenance fell under their jurisdiction. The encroachment of the Federal government into this area was cloaked in a Supreme Court ruling that said that "When the power to establish post offices and post roads was surrendered to Congress it was a complete power, and the grant carried with it the right to exercise all the powers which made that power effective." This interpretation required finesse, for unfortunately, although the states did not want to relinquish authority for roads, at the same time they were hard pressed to pay for the necessary improvements.

Resolving this issue required a great deal of give-and-take ... and time ... and patience. There were several ways that an equitable resolution was possible. One option was for Uncle Sam to pay the costs of road building through a form of state aid, while the states retained their rights to construct and maintain the roads using Federal money any way they liked. Another option called for the Federal government to build a basic nationwide network of highways, around which the states could connect their local roads. A third option called for the states and Federal government to share the costs of road building.

During the first decade of this century, beginning with the nation's first "good road" bill, a stillborn piece of legislation known as the Bronlow-Latimer bill, which failed to make it out of committee in 1903, a steady stream of unsuccessful Federal legislation tried to incorporate each of these ideas.

The difficulty was not deciding on how to split the bill, but how to resolve the matter of local versus Federal responsibility. The debate struck at all levels. For farm families, and the National Grange that represented many of them, good roads were a must. But even among Grange chapters, as with

18

the public at large, there was uncertainty over the responsibility of county, state and Federal governments.

Oliver Wilson, master of the National Grange in 1913, emphasized the growing shift in responsibility for road work in his annual address to his membership. "The public highway is a matter of general concern," he said. "The old idea that the country road should be constructed and maintained by the farmers has been disapproved. It is now recognized that good roads are of as much importance to the consumer as to the producer, as anything that lessens the cost of transportation is a benefit to the consumer."

Ultimately a partnership emerged. By 1891, some states were pressing for Federal assistance in funding for road construction. By then, many states had already created their own highway departments and there was a call for the establishment of a Federal agency to coordinate the nation's disjointed road building efforts.

A bad road in Tennessee. The most expensive road the community could afford.

An example of poor drainage. Water drained from the high ground on each side and transformed the whole road into a ditch.

Two years later a government panel of inquiry was convened and an Office of Public Roads was established within the Department of Agriculture. The inquiry was backed by a $10,000 appropriation. The panel's mandate was to examine "the systems of road management throughout the United States, to make investigations in regard to the best methods of road making, to prepare publications on the subject suitable for distribution, and to assist the agricultural colleges and experiment stations in disseminating information on this subject." State

and local leaders long realized that they could not act alone. But at the Federal level little money was allocated for roads. Although the Office of Public Roads was a turn-of-the-century creation it received less than $1 during its first 15 years of existence. This advisory bureau had little real power. For the most part, it acted more like a cheerleading group than anything else. But, to its credit, it did bring state and Federal officials together to talk, if nothing else. Such dialogue was essential. It ultimately provided the groundwork for later efforts.

From such discussion came the convening of a "National Good Roads Convention" at Des Moines, Iowa, in October 1899. Out of this meeting came a resolution that called for better cooperation between the Federal and state governments. According to the resolution:

> The postal system of the General Government was instituted upon the theory of serving without discrimination all the people in a just and liberal manner, and recognizing the many social and pecuniary advantages of rural free mail service not only to the rural population but also to all classes, and that such service is dependent on good roads: Therefore, Resolved, That we are in favor of such an appropriation by Congress as will ensure the speedy and permanent establishment of such service throughout the country where the conditions as to good roads and population will justify, and that we hereby respectfully request our members of Congress in both the Senate and House to vote for such an appropriation.

This was an affirmation of the desire by both state and Federal agencies to cooperate, but it did not resolve the issue of states' rights. Nor did it provide any concrete details about how the state and Federal governments were to work together, other than the fact that Uncle Sam was expected to foot some, or all, of the bill.

Between 1897 and 1908 local governments spent approximately $72 million on bridges, culverts and other improvements. In one county in Indiana, farmers themselves paid over $2,600 to grade and gravel a road in order to qualify for RFD.

By 1901, 18 bridges had been built and over $32,000 spent in road repairs in Massachusetts, Connecticut, New York, New Jersey and Pennsylvania, in order to obtain Rural Free Delivery. In Texas, 100 fords were bridged and 10 stone bridges were erected over previously impassable streams for the same reason. In Iowa, Washington, Minnesota, and California, agreements were made between county commissioners and special agents of the Rural Free Delivery service to open, repair, and maintain country roads.

A few years later, at another "good roads" gathering in St. Louis, President Theodore Roosevelt focused on an equally important reason for Federal and state cooperation—the need to stem the alarming numbers of young people fleeing the isolation of the family farms. "It is a fine thing to see our cities built up, but not at the expense of the country districts .... We cannot expect the ablest, the most eager, the most ambitious young men to stay in the country, to stay on the farm, unless there are certain advantages," he told the group, adding, "Farm life is in too many cases a life of isolation, a life in which it is a matter of great and real difficulty for

A good road in Durham, North Carolina. More than 100 miles of these roads were built without increasing the rate of taxation.

one to communicate with their neighbors." Roosevelt's prognosis for the future was bleakly optimistic: "You can rest assured that, unless this is changed, there will be a tendency to leave the farms on the part of those very people whom we should most wish to see stay there."

Congressman Ezekiel S. Chandler saw better roads as a way of stemming the migration of young people from the nation's agricultural centers. "The perfect country road would go far towards working such a change, in that social visiting and communication which under present conditions is exceptional," wrote the Mississippian in 1912.

Well maintained roads enhanced the social lives of those living in rural communities by ensuring that people were no longer homebound for weeks due to inclement weather. Good roads also reportedly had a positive impact upon land values. According to a Post Office Department study, during the first decade of this century farm values increased as a result of RFD. For example, in New York state valuations attributable to mail service rose from one to 200 percent during that 10-year span. In New Jersey the increase was two to five percent and in Delaware it was five to 60 percent. In the New England states the increases ranged from two to 55 percent. How much farm values would have increased normally was not reported.

It was estimated that the price per acre was 25 percent higher when the farm had access to a macadamized road than when it was off a questionably maintained dirt road. The total number of miles of macadamized roads steadily increased during the first decade of this century. By 1908, New York state, which was considered a leader in the road improvement campaign, had 1,342 miles of macadam roads, yet as impressive as this may appear, it still only represented about one mile of macadam for each rural carrier in the state. Maine, with 441 carriers, had only 30 miles of macadam; New Hampshire, with 215 carriers, had 51 miles; and Vermont, with 324 carriers, had 72 miles. Massachusetts, with 270 RFD routes, had 887 miles that were macadamized; while Connecticut, with almost the same number of carriers as Massachusetts, had only about one-fourth of its macadam miles. New Jersey came close to matching Massachusetts' proportions. The remaining miles within each state were gravel, earth, or sand in dry seasons.

Although statistically, the amount of macadamized surfaces doesn't really seem like it represents a massive paving spree, it does reflect an evolving pattern of improvements being made, which was expanded in subsequent decades.

A well-maintained rural road in Montgomery, Alabama.

Good roads were also seen as a universal conduit to commerce. Unlike the railroads, which extracted enormous rates for hauling freight, paved roads provided ways to cheaply move products to market anytime the seller wished. It also ensured that markets could be supplied far from the source of supply. In time, this would give rise to the nation's highway trucking industry, but in the early 1900s this was only a vision.

Congressman Chandler's vision for nationally paved rural roads, and his concern for rural migration, prompted him to introduce two bills related to the construction of a national system of public roads in 1912. Chandler believed that Congressional appropriations over the past few decades for river, railway and harbor projects, efforts made largely at the expense of road building, had been abused; this represented lard bucket politics at their worst. Members of congress with harbors or waterways in their district spent and spent on improvements that would keep the voters back home happy.

Illinois Senator Lawrence Y. Sherman was appalled by the gluttony. He made up this pork barrel poem and delivered it during a debate on a typical harbors and rivers bill:

"Every one can see by the dawn's early light that millions that gleam in the logroller's sight, while the creeks and the bayous and frog ponds galore make the taxpayers swear and feel painfully sore, the sandbars and sawyers, the snags and the scows, the congressmen's schemes and the engineer's rows, the dredges and shovels, the dikes and the dams spend enough cash to break two Uncle Sams. The troop blithely gather from hill and from plain, from mountain peaks, snowcapped again and again, down from alkali dust, from sagebrush and pine, they gather their cohorts, line upon line; they move down together, one seems but a dab, but when all march along to the loot step of grab, a fearsome procession gaining strength as they come, it's the International Worker World's, the bolshevists bum of all legislation that unravels our roll, depletes our exchequer and gravels our soul, hangs on the majestical rivers that flow from the far north and their mantles of snow, that run by the wheat field and the corn in its rows and ripples along where the cotton boll blows; they sap and they burden, they dog and deface the Great Father of Waters in gratifying disgraces; their impudent face in desert and swamp is everywhere seen as they brazenly romp from valley to sea, from prairie to lake as the rivers and harbors the lawmakers rake."

Congressmen without such waterway projects lavished their hometown folks with massive post office and courthouse projects. Together, these highly visible projects kept constituents happy at the cost of hundreds of millions of dollars annually, but pitifully little had been spent on roads.

Advocates of river and harbor initiatives believed that not less than $50 million was needed annually to reasonably complete major projects. At that rate, over the next 20 years the national treasury would have forked over a staggering $1 billion. As it was,

A chert gravel road in Chattanooga, Tennessee, in 1910.

21

Representative Ezekiel S. Chandler, Jr., of Mississippi.

by 1911 nearly $700 million had already been spent since the first such appropriations had been made 125 years earlier. Many lawmakers reasoned that some fair share of Federal funds was needed for good roads.

In response, a good roads committee was created by Congress in 1913, with Missouri Congressman Dorsey W. Shackleford at the helm. This committee was expected to create a bumper crop of pork barrel projects. Such anticipation led *R.F.D. News* to predict in its June 7, 1913, issue: "The amount of money to be appropriated under the committee's authorization ... is enormous and the fight for local roads will make political gossip from now on." Unfortunately, like all such "gossip" there was more fiction than fact behind it.

Former President William Howard Taft, for one, took exception to creating yet another drain from the Federal trough. "The evils of pork barrel legislation with the mad chase for good roads money are largely caused by pseudo reformers inspired by a feeling that they want to take from those who have and give to those who haven't," he told a crowd during a weekly lecture at Yale University.

This prompted a hot reply from George Diehl, chairman of the American Automobile Association's Good Roads Board. "It would appear that the former head of the nation has not given the good roads question the thorough consideration which it deserves," Diehl asserted. "In view of the facts, and in view of the tremendous savings in money and energy which always follows the construction of good roads, how can there be any question but that the construction of a system of great national highways connecting the large centers of population and the state capitals, would not benefit the whole country by the development of its producers and marketing facilities?" claimed Diehl.

Some in Congress, lawmakers such as Ezekiel Chandler, agreed with Diehl. They doubted the wisdom of a double standard. He thought ill of such selective largess. If harbor and river projects were prime pork, so should roads and bridges be, he reckoned. Congressman Chandler's view was that as things then stood, it was unfair to farm families. "Why should farmers pay for making rivers more navigable and harbors deeper and more spacious if these improvements do not help haul products to market?" he asked his colleagues. And, how is it that the United States had the finest railways— made possible largely with government help—yet also had the poorest highways in the world? he wondered. "In the first 50 or 60 years after the foundation of the government something like $14,000,000,000 was appropriated for the building and maintenance of railways .... But almost from the very beginning of the railway era appropriations for public highways became conspicuous by their absence."

With prior legislative emphasis on supporting waterways and harbors, and with railways well established in the private sector, thanks to an array of Federal perks, lawmakers seemed to think that there was no further need for any comparable transportation infrastructure. Chandler, however, was convinced that good roads were as important, if not more so, than waterways. The problem was that his initiatives came at a time when the nation was growing tired of wasteful spending. The last thing Americans were in the mood for was another attack on the Federal treasury, especially one as astronomically expensive as building roads.

Despite the odds, Chandler and other lawmakers pressed for meaningful annual appropriations. His first concern was to get Federally funded road construction projects started. One of Chandler's 1912 bills called for the Federal appropriation of $100 million to match state funds for building the national road system; however, the appropriation that Chandler envisioned fell far short of what the states were already doing on their own. Chandler believed that the states were already doing their part, but that "The National Government, however, thus far lags ingloriously in the rear."

The philosophy of another ardent congressional leader, Ohio Representative William B. Francis, was equally simple: "Show me a country traversed by many easy and pleasant highways and I will show you a country of intelligence, prosperity and contentment, abounding in accessible schools and

There was no way in the world that one person could have been able to push his way out of this mess.

churches, improved and valuable lands." The alternative, he said, was a "country segregated from civilization, too often abounding in ignorance."

If our grandfathers used Francis' viewpoint as a gauge, the United States was indeed backwards—and road-wise it was! Judging from the conditions of roads in Francis' day—and well before—the United States could well have been viewed as a place of neglect and poverty. Our backwoods roads, and our few highways, were deplorable, and much of the world knew it.

Since the founding of the republic, foreigners were constantly appalled by American travel. This was true when Lieutenant Fred Fitzgerald DeRoos toured the United States in 1826. In his illustrated *Personal Narrative*, which was published in London the following year, he was none too flattering about his experiences while traveling over one of the best roads in America. "It matters little to the American driver, where he sits. He is indeed in all respects a far different personage from his great-coated prototype in England. He is in general extremely dexterous in the art of driving, though his costume is of a most grotesque description. Figure to yourself a slipshod sloven, dressed in a striped calico jacket, and an old straw hat, alternately arranging the fragile harness of his horses, and springing again upon his box with surprising agility; careless of the bones of his passengers, and confident in his skill and resources, he scruples not frequently to gallop his coach over corduroy roads (so called for being formed of the trunks of trees laid transversely side-by-side along the length of the roadbed) or dash it round corners and through holes that would appall the heart of the stoutest English coachman, however elated with gin, or irritated by opposition," wrote DeRoos.

Such comments were still true nearly a century later when another English traveler observed in 1912: "In the United States, roads as they are known in the Old World exist only within the purlieus of the well-established cities. Once beyond these boundaries, the highway gives way to an ill-defined track, full of holes, with its surface a stratum of treacherous dust, inches in thickness in summer and little more than a quagmire and pools of slime in the wet weather."

Americans weren't typically offended by such unflattering comments because they were true. Besides, Americans were doing plenty of badmouthing on their own, including Congressman William Francis, who favored a massive road building campaign, such as the idea championed by another senator to build seven great national highways leading to the nation's capital. The scheme, estimated to cost $148 million, called for two great routes to cross the entire continent, another to run the length of the Atlantic coast, and others to link the nation's major cities. Around the great skeleton, states and local communities were to make subsequent connections. But once again, the question in developing such a highway system was how to sell it to the states.

Some, like Congressman Stanton Warburton of Washington, favored linking good roads to the national defense. Nobody could possibly balk at that, he thought, especially since the country was already tied up with the issue of military preparedness. But the congressman went a bit further. Realizing that the government was face to face with a serious problem of raising sufficient money to pay for increased armaments, one senator dreamed of a system of "National Military Roads" paid for by smokers. A small tax, too small to even be noticed, thought Warburton, was to be charged. "I propose to raise the funds by bestowing the Internal Revenue Tax of 1879 on tobacco and set aside the additional income from the source as a national road fund," said the lawmaker in 1913. He envisioned a 15,000-mile system, built at a cost of $20,000 a mile. Such "sin taxes" weren't at all popular among the nation's smoking population, which was formidable at that time.

There were other false starts. One of the most sweeping proposals to come before Congress was championed by Oregon Senator Jonathan Bourne, just before he was voted out of office. His plan called for $3 billion in funds, one-third for construction projects, and the remainder for maintenance costs doled out on a yearly basis. The billion-dollar construction funds were to be apportioned to the states based upon their physical size, population, road mileage, and tax base. In exchange for the funds, which were basically long-term loans, 50-year state bonds were required as collateral. These were to yield four percent interest.

Bourne openly admitted that "The expenditure of $3 billion by the government and the several states for highway improvements is at first thought, a startling proposition." But, he added, "When we consider the magnitude of the intervention affected, it will be seen as a wise investment." If, Bourne rea-

Senator Jonathan Bourne of Oregon.

soned, the cost of road construction increased property values by as little as three percent, the plan would yield more than it cost, given the fact that the nation then had about 890 million acres of farmland.

The *Washington Post* sided with Bourne. It editorialized: "Although the plan evolved by former Senator Jonathan Bourne, Jr., contemplates an ultimate expenditure of $3 billion, a successful system of improved public roads for this country cannot be had at less cost. The bigness of the scheme, therefore, should not weigh against it." But it did.

One positive outcome of the Bourne plan was the appropriation of $500,000 for roads in 1913. Despite the fact that it was far less than Bourne had hoped, this was viewed as a major coup, one that was said to represent the largest amount appropriated for roads since Henry Clay pulled off the funding for the National Road generations earlier.

The push to improve the nation's roads in the 1890s sprang from a number of factors, including the growing political influence of rural Americans, the need to bring produce in from farmlands to markets as quickly and cheaply as possible, the introduction of the automobile, the creation and rapid expansion of rural mail service, and the growing popularity of bicycling.

Better roads also meant that farm products could be delivered to markets while prices remained high, if delivered at all. The Department of Agriculture estimated that a significant amount of crops remained on the farms each year because of poor roads. Figures ran as high as one-third of all farm products were held back from market in this way. As a result of studies done by leading farm economists in the 1910s, the losses amounted to about $3 million annually. The Department of Agriculture calculated that "on the basis of these figures ... if the roads of the country were put into better shape and properly maintained it would be possible for farmers to get to shipping points at all seasons of the year, and in this way one-third of the crop harvested would not remain on the farms to go to waste, as at present."

Improved roads had other positive domino effects. It also saved time and wear and tear in getting to and from one place and another: teams of horses did not get as fatigued hauling heavy loads, wagons and harnesses did not have to be repaired as often, children could get to school easier, farm families could attend church or Grange lectures or political gatherings more often, and mail could be conveniently delivered.

In order to obtain a rural mail route, rural Americans had to work together. This wasn't often hard for farm families, who despite their great personal pride, had a keen sense of "neighborliness" when it came to collective tasks. Perhaps the impact of having to work together was the most difficult for rural hamlets and villages. Like farm families along mail routes, these local communities had to ensure that the path over which the mail would move was passable at all times and under all types of adverse weather conditions. Obstacles such as gates and tree stumps had to be removed, creeks had to be fordable or bridged, and the road bed kept reasonably smooth. Affected communities had to work collectively together to adequately drain washouts and properly grade ruts. They also had to forget town rivalries and work together, and perhaps even more painfully, pool their labor or meager financial resources to solve collective problems that would threaten the all-important link to the outside.

If a road should fall into disrepair once a mail route was established, the local postmaster would have to see to it that the necessary repairs were made. To help in this, postmasters were directed to tell residents along the affected route that "It is the hope of the department that the patrons who are receiving the benefits of the service appreciate it, and that they will promptly cooperate in an effort to repair all deficient portions."

In this respect, some communities naturally had it better than others. According to carrier T.S. Burch from Caruthersville, Missouri, "This is a part of Heaven. We are down in the Mississippi Valley, 100 miles south of Cairo, Illinois, and 100 miles north of Memphis, Tennessee. The valley is as level as a floor, and our roads, for eight months in the year cannot be beat. The soil is a black, sandy loam, no sand blows. They become smooth and hard in spring, summer and fall." Winter was another story!

Most portions of the country had poor road conditions. "I have about three miles of shell (paved) roads, about nine miles of sandy roads, and the balance of the 21.1 (mile route) is mud and water," said Virginia carrier George Fentress in 1908.

At this time, the usual method of road building and maintenance consisted of going over the road bed with a horse-drawn split-log drag. These homemade devices acted much like a modern-day road grader. Drags consisted of two seven to nine foot logs, roughly 12 inches in diameter, with the scraping edge flat to the front. The logs were set on an angle about 30 inches apart and fastened together with three strong braces. The entire contraption was dragged by horses from a doubletree and chains. It gathered all of the muck and rubbish into the sides.

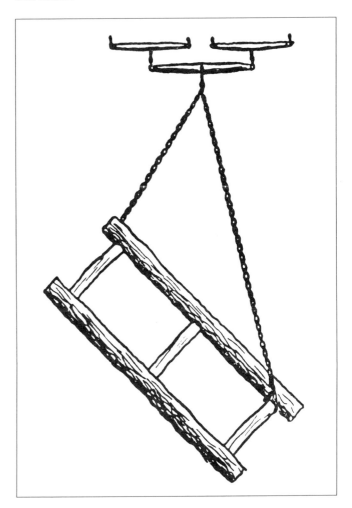

Drawing of a typical split-log drag.

25

I LOVE MY DEEP WATERWAYS, BUT, OH, YOU GOOD ROADS!

An editorial cartoon published in a 1910 issue of R.F.D. News *to focus attention to the need to drag rural roads.*

As primitive as it seems, the split-log drag was considered the best road building device in use at the time by the Department of Agriculture. Before the turn of the century paving was an expensive proposition that was seldom used. Often, crushed stone, shells, or gravel were used to make roadbeds firmer. Some local communities went all out to make their roads as passable as possible. At the urging of carrier George DeKoven, Baraboo, Wisconsin, replaced its crude split-log drag it had been using to scrape roadbeds with a fancy steam roller. Other localities paved their roads to ensure all-weather travel, although this was a relative luxury.

Some believed that roads were strictly something between the states and the local communities. The view of Laurens Enos, the president of the American Automobile Association, was that: "To ask the national government to do that which properly devolves upon the local community is basically wrong and untenable. Our government is composed of state units; the source to which the community should appeal is the state, which in turn should go to the Federal fountain head for cooperation along lines which are inter-state and otherwise sufficiently general to justify the employment of national funds." Speaking in 1913, Enos noted that "to call upon the national government to deal with local units direct, and ignoring the state governments, is procedurally contrary to Constitutional rights and common sense."

Actually, Federal officials realized this all too well. They knew that American road improvements took teamwork. In an effort to improve roads the Post Office Department, and other Federal agencies, brokered deal after deal with the Bureau of Public Roads with state highway offices, as well as local road supervisors and county commissioners. Most times the deal making was congenial, as in the case of Giles County, Tennessee, where the local legislature enacted an ordinance that reclassified the county's roads as public highways that required all obstructions, such as gates, be removed so that mail carriers could travel the entire length of each route unimpeded. Other times, severe arm twisting

A well-maintained rural road in Montgomery, Alabama.

The same section of road after being dragged for 30 minutes.

was required. But most of these efforts were isolated attempts aimed at gaining some degree of cooperation between the Federal government and the states. Some sort of cooperative working relationship needed to be forged, one that could work in all of the states, without the use of intimidation. By now Federal officials fully realized that they needed to deal directly with the states, leaving the local communities alone whenever possible.

In 1915, Congressman Dorsey W. Shackleford, the chairman of the House Committee on Roads, thought that perhaps the time was right to create such a cooperative Federal/state relationship. He was adamant that "the need for an adequate road law in the country is an urgent one," and he acted on that belief by introducing legislation calling for the use of $25 million for all manner of road building. When nothing happened in 1915, Shackleford

pushed even harder in 1916. Unfortunately, the outlook at the beginning of 1916 was bleak. In February, *R.F.D. News* told its readers "The present outlook for good roads legislation is gloomier than it has been since the improved highway agitation became acute."

Shackleford thought otherwise. He was certain that now was the time to act. "In times past when the volume and weight of postal matter were negligible the interest of the general government in the condition of the roads was not substantial," he argued, "but with the advent of rural free delivery came a Federal necessity for better roads, and with the now rapidly expanding parcel post, that necessity has become acute."

His 1916 bill gave a great deal of flexibility to the Secretary of Agriculture to decide how best to divide the funds appropriated under the act, but there were limits. He could only deal with state governments, not townships, committees or districts. This discretionary power was necessary since "The states differed so widely in climate and terrain, as well as legislative restraints," observed Shackleford.

By 1916, the nation enjoyed over 2.4 million miles of roads outside of incorporated areas. Unfortunately, only about 11 percent of those miles were paved in some fashion or another. Of the different forms of hard-surfacing (macadam, brick, concrete, or negligible other types), macadam was the most common. Over 10,000 miles of macadam roads existed by the time the United States was drawn into World War I. (The spelling probably should be "MacAdam" in honor of its inventor, Scotsman John Loudon MacAdam, who devised a method of binding small rocks into a bituminous mixture in the early 19th century.)

In only a half year of 1916, the cumulative impact of the good roads movement, prodded in large part by America's desire for rural free delivery, provided the groundwork for passage of the long awaited highway legislation. Signed into law on July 11 by President Woodrow Wilson, the "Good Roads Bill," the first measure providing for Federal and state cooperation, authorized the use of $85 million in Federal funds over a five-year period, provided the states matched Uncle Sam's level of funding on a dollar-for-dollar basis. Also known as the "Federal Aid Road Act," the 1916 legislation was largely the brainchild of Representative Shackleford of Missouri. Within a few days of being signed into law, $5 million worth of good roads money was being allocated to the states. Disbursements ranged from $291,000 for Texas to $8,000 for Delaware.

One of the earliest concrete bridges constructed in Massachusetts.

A major improvement. A relocated road near Greensboro, North Carolina.

From the start, Shackleford's hope was to somehow bend the two opposing factors that had kept the Federal government and the states at odds for so long. Shackleford's view that "Roads are local concerns, and primarily it is the duty of the States to provide for their people," but that "To carry and deliver the mail is a function of the Federal government, and it is its duty to provide itself with the facilities necessary to a proper performance of this function" prevailed. His proposal was an amalgamation of those otherwise opposing thoughts.

In this respect, his aim was to strike a happy medium between the states and the Federal government, and he succeeded. To his lasting credit, Shackleford's measure included the requirement that "the United States ... shall aid the states in the construction and maintenance of rural post roads" and that "all construction and maintenance of roads ... shall be under the supervision of the state highway departments," using funds obtained from both state and Federal coffers. This effectively ended the century old debate over whether or not the states or the Federal government would call the shots on the majority of the nation's road building projects, depending on which one foot the bill.

In concluding things this way, Congress dodged the issue of "pork barrelism." Arguably, there really wasn't any real "pork" in the road laws because the Federal government and the states were footing the bills, a fact that prompted George C. Diehl of the Good Roads Board of the American Automobile Association to remark that "The most refreshing feature of the Federal Aid Road Act is its freedom from the taint of 'pork barrel.'" This, he thought, was an automatic check upon any raid on the United States Treasury, and besides, it was further safeguarded by the fact that the states were not likely to squander their own money. Under normal circumstances there typically were no such assurances when the Federal government was paying the entire price of totally government-sponsored "pork" projects. But most important, this particular outcome laid the foundation upon which much of our modern highway system is based.

EVOLUTIONS

SOAP BOXES WON'T DO

When Rural Free Delivery started as an experiment on October 1, 1896, nobody knew how long it would last. The frugal farmers along the first rural routes in West Virginia were not willing to spend good money on mailboxes in case the whole scheme proved to be a flash in the pan. Lard cans, feed boxes, and other secondhand crates were fine for starters, but the jumble of soap and cigar boxes created a pathetic roadside spectacle, one that was characterized as "so much variety and inharmony [sic]." In typical "government-ese" the Post Office Department declared that this hodgepodge "detracted from the tone of the general system and gave it anything but the appearance of a Government institution."

Being a government institution, the Post Office Department tried to encourage uniformity wherever possible. Up until the early 1900s, homemade boxes were okay, but commercial boxes were clearly the preferred choice of the postal service. A committee was convened in 1901 to examine all of the different boxes available on the open market and to "pass judgment upon the merits of the different makes."

The committee's approved specifications for commercial boxes were somewhat loose: All boxes had to be produced "in the best workmanlike manner." Seams and joints had to be well-constructed so that rain, snow, or dust would not get into the box when the lid was closed. Boxes were to be made from sheet metal, and galvanized if possible. Rectangular boxes were to be at least 18 by 6 by 6 inches in size; cylindrical boxes were to be not less than 18 by 6 inches. Boxes opening from the side or top were preferred over those opening from the ends. All boxes had to have an adjustable and durable metallic signal that would show when mail was inside.

Each box had to be erected by the roadside so that the carrier could have easy access without dismounting from his vehicle.

The group selected boxes from 14 manufacturers. On March 16, 1901, the committee's decisions were announced by way of letters to the lucky firms. This made for sweet reading for company officials: "I have the honor to inform you that the Postmaster General has approved the report of the Committee recommending the adoption in the Rural Free Delivery Service (of) the box submitted by you."

Whenever possible, postal officials preferred uniformity. Although they could not force farmers on the same routes to all buy the same style of box, they desired that "boxes on each route should be of uniform construction." After 1901, the boxes on new routes were to be from one of the 14 approved firms.

Unfortunately, not all postal patrons purchased commercial boxes. Many holdouts simply made their own, which prompted one manufacturer to observe that many of the homemade versions were "better fitted for rat traps or puzzles for the insane." Depending on the size and style, these commercially produced boxes were priced from 50 cents to several dollars, including small locks. The Post Office Department's position on this was that "Unless the boxes erected on new routes are of approved patterns, they will not be served by rural carriers."

"[All of them] are of about as much account as a lard can with the lid taken off."

With so many manufacturers out there, deciding on which box to buy was a tough decision. An expert opinion was usually welcome. And, since the carriers were more often as not someone from

One of the approved mailbox designs, as advertised in 1903.

the neighborhood, someone who the local folks trusted, their opinions carried a great deal of weight. Rural patrons relied on their carriers for advice, and the manufacturers capitalized on this trust, offering carriers' lucrative commissions for hawking their boxes.

This sideline didn't sit well with postal officials who quickly nipped the practice in the bud. Soliciting sales soon became improper conduct for carriers. The rule forbidding this sort of thing was crystal clear: "Officials and employees of the Post Office Department and postal service shall not act as agents for manufacturers of rural mailboxes and shall not be interested, directly or indirectly, in the manufacture or sale of any rural mailbox."

As a comeback, many mailbox makers offered to pay carriers for suggesting others who could do the same thing. "If you have a friend who can canvass your route, let him write us. We will pay him liberally for his work," announced the Signal Mailbox Co. in 1908.

At the same time, carriers were offered what amounted to finders' fees for giving manufacturers "insider" information about new routes. Like other firms, the Signal Mailbox Co. tried this approach, advertising in *R.F.D. News*: "Do you know of any new routes being petitioned for? We pay cash for such information." Such tips gave makers a jump on the competition. The goal was to sell a mailbox to every family on the proposed route before anyone else could.

The willingness to obtain a mailbox became the covenant for service. Postal officials made it clear that in order to establish service a prescribed

One example of an approved rural mailbox on A.T. Dubendorff's route from Bronson, Michigan. Dubendorff used a two-speed 1910 Wagner motorcycle.

number of families had to qualify "as patrons either by erecting approved boxes on the proposed line of travel or filing written agreements that they will join with others in the use of boxes." Without such assurances, no route was authorized.

By 1913, a great many different styles of mailboxes were available, but few were able to accommodate large-sized parcels, a major concern with the advent of parcel post. This prompted the postal service to create a committee to design the perfect mailbox. For nearly a year the group examined all of the different models currently available, plus alternative designs from inventors and manufacturers; but none was right.

Although an array of different styles was available, letter carriers were not really pleased with any of them. At the 1916 convention of the National Association of Rural Letter Carriers, delegate John B. Newcomer protested: "I have mailboxes galore, the likes of which I will get no more .... [They] are of about as much account as a lard can with the lid taken off."

Frequently these boxes were simply too small to hold all of the mail. The average rural mailbox was about big enough to hold several letters, a small package, and a wrapped newspaper. When a parcel was too large to fit in a patron's box a small "Could-not-deliver" card was left instead. The card explained how the patron could pick up the parcel at the post office. Another arrangement was to leave the package in a larger box at the base of the letterbox.

Carriers universally thought that some of the existing "approved" boxes, such as the Bates-Hawley, Beaver, and Hessler models, were too small. The fact that so many different types of boxes were "approved" perplexed carriers such as Newcomer. "I have numerous boxes—or quite a number of them—that have no names on them at all and they are just merely stamped 'Approved by the Postmaster General.' I don't know whether he ever saw those boxes or ever heard of them or how they got that stamp on them but if he did approve them he surely does not understand the Rural Free Delivery Service and what [carriers] have to contend with," the Maryland delegate told his colleagues.

Before 1915, rural mailboxes appeared in almost every shape and size imaginable. This prompted the Post Office Department to design its own box. The now familiar tunnel-shaped box was designed in 1915 by postal engineer Roy Joroleman. "Everyone had an idea as to what to use for a rural mailbox with the result that I was asked to design a box," recorded Joroleman in his journal.

To encourage widespread acceptance and availability, Joroleman's design was not patentable. Nor were restrictions set upon the box's manufacture or sale. Local postmasters were even furnished with lists of manufacturers and prices of the new boxes.

An early tilt-top mailbox, manufactured by the American Mail Box Company in the early 1900s.

Two sizes of Joroleman's tunnel-shaped box were ultimately designed. The smaller size was for ordinary letter mail, while the larger size was for all classes of mail, including parcel post. Patrons were not immediately required to discard existing boxes. Older style boxes could be used as long as they remained functional; but, after July 1, 1916, only the newer style could be installed.

This edict often got carriers into hot water with their customers. One reported how he was instructed to tell six families to fix their faulty mailboxes, which they did. Six months later he was told to tell them to make more repairs or replace them within 30 days or service would be stopped. For conveying the message, "I came pretty near to getting lynched," the carrier said.

"Leave me som stamps, meny as it will get."

For most of us, in our day-to-day lives, a mailbox is simply a tool for communication between one correspondent and another. But sometimes, a mailbox can be used as a means of communication between the customer and the carrier. In Easter of 1913, the members of each family on Milton Rumbeck's route left him an egg. When the Kansas carrier tallied up his 1913 gifts he had 528 eggs.

More often than not such carrier and customer mailbox-based communications centered around asking for favors, the most popular being requests for stamps. Such requests were always accompanied by one of the worst, most horrid nuisances ... "fishing" for pennies. This was especially difficult in the winter when the coins left to pay for postage would freeze to the bottom of the box or get lodged in the crevices. This nuisance prompted postal officials to insist that coin-holders be incorporated into boxes, but practically nobody took such instructions seriously. "Penny fishing" got to be such a universal joke that a poem was written in 1908 on the subject. The poem is still understood by carriers today:

> It's all right in the springtime,
> Or when summer breezes blow,
> But a different proposition,
> When it's thirty-two below;
> When all your fingers and your toes,
> Are frozen hard as rocks,
> It's most anything but funny,
> Scratching pennies from the box!

During our grandfathers' era people seem to have thought more in terms of pennies than we do today. Nowadays, if it probably weren't for the fact that we have to buy things for $1.99, or some equally silly price, instead of $2 ... or for buying postage stamps at odd rates, such as 29 cents ... as a nation, we probably could wean ourselves of our need for pennies. In any event, in years gone by pennies seem to have been more a mental basis for making financial transactions than they are now. This fact led some rural carriers to commonly play a wicked little joke on their patrons. The scenario went like this: When a patron met them at the box to buy a single stamp the carrier would lean out of his mail wagon, as if to confide some sinister secret, and offer to sell 13 two-cent stamps for one cent and a quarter. Many customers reacted as though this was a real deal, questioning how such a bargain was possible. And, occasionally a patron would even complain to the local postmaster that the carrier was fixing to cheat Uncle Sam by discounting the price of stamps.

There was another side to this penny problem. Some carriers actually preferred digging for pennies rather than facing the alternatives, at least that was Stacy Taft's viewpoint. "I would rather get two pennies out of the box any time than to have some woman [and her baby] meet me at the box," he said. According to his telling of things, she'd ask for a stamp and then lick all of the adhesive off between her gossiping ... and then she'd complain because the stamp wouldn't stick to the envelope. "And then when you remind her [that] she has not paid you for it [she'll ask] if you will just hold the baby while she runs to get [the change]. Then your trouble begins .... Any time I would rather get two pennies out of a box than hold [a] kid."

I don't know if exchanging pennies for "real" money is any more troublesome today than in years past. Most Americans probably have some place where pennies are relegated ... a coffee can, bowl, or the bottom of some drawer. Like his modern day counterparts, one Illinois carrier, Walter Bartlett of Jerseyville, was sort of a penny pack rat. He would squirrel away his penny cache until the end of the year. His 1915 accumulation amounted to 12,400 one-cent coins. At year's end, he took them by wheelbarrow to the post office for conversion to paper money. He figured his load was about 62 pounds of copper.

This age-old problem was what carrier P.H. Schran called his "greatest trouble" in 1908, but it became even more unpleasant and time consuming as stamp prices began to rise. Two decades ago an Oklahoma patron's request was "Please leave 10 thirteen cent stamps. They cost $1.30. There is 80 cents in this sack and two quarters. You be sure to count them. I have counted them twice. If there is not 80 pennies I will pay you tomorrow. But I think it is correct." Unwilling to bank on having counted the money twice, the buyer counted the one cent coins once again. This was enough to convince her that it was all there. Scribbling further down on the handwritten slip of torn paper was the self-assured note: "There is 80 pennies in the sack!"

A few years later a similar request read: "A $10 [bill] and 13 cents is in this envelop (sic). Leave me som (sic) stamps, [as] meny (sic) as it will get."

"By the time I got my blouse half ripped off and the lizard out, I was over on the grass."

It's easy to forget that you owe someone money, especially if it's pocket change. Years ago Ann Landers published a letter from the wife of a letter carrier who wished the syndicated writer to know how often carriers fork out money from their own pockets. In her husband's case, the charity often ran as much as $2 a day. "You'd be surprised, Ann, if you knew how many people don't even say 'Thank you,' much less pay the letter carrier what they owe," the writer noted. The published letter had an impact. Many carriers found small notes

Small boxes, such as this one from the Bond Steel Post Company, were not well-suited for large parcels.

asking for forgiveness in mailboxes. Wesley Clark, who served as a Connecticut carrier from 1948 to 1984, kept one of the notes he received. The note, with a nickel taped inside, read "This column reminded me I owed you a nickel for a postage due letter."

Where there was a language barrier between a customer and a carrier, the mailbox was the place where translations took place. Sometimes such difficulty in communications was resolved through the use of drawings of what was wanted. In other cases sales catalogs became the medium

for communicating desires. Ed Thibodeaux remembers his father using catalogs along his route from Cut Off to Golden Meadow, Louisiana. His father was a rural carrier when Ed was born in 1909. Ed recalls how "Few natives spoke or wrote English, always Cajun French. My dad never spoke French. They met him with a mail order catalog and pointed to what they wanted in the catalog and he filled out the order for them."

This kind of special service hasn't disappeared. It remains very much a part of rural mail service. "I love the people on my route," says Carol Varn, who is typical of those working today. "They are a part of my family and I really care for most of them."

That caring shows itself in many ways. For Varn, it is reflected in the countless ways "we have seen each other through many happy occasions, such as marriages and births, and also sad times, such as the loss of a husband or wife." It also is demonstrated time and again in little ways, such as the special way she delivered one lady's first Social Security check. She was looking for it everyday for a couple of weeks. When it finally arrived, Varn put a big red ribbon on the outside of the envelope and delivered the check to the retiree's front door.

During Peggy Ludwig's 15 years as a rural carrier in Marriottsville, Maryland, one of her customers wrote a series of "Roses are Red" poems. In 1983, she received this installment:

Roses are red
Violets are blue,
We have a new mailbox
Just for you.
We have a post
That you have found,
It looks to us
To be sturdy and sound.
The post and the mailbox
We plan to mate.
The end result
Will be just great.
The solution we have
I'm sure you will hail,
Nothing is too good
for the U.S. Mail.

Actually, the owners were somewhat prodded into erecting the new mailbox with a subtle hint from Ludwig. The old mailbox was so ramshackle that Ludwig left the family a new mailbox post as an indication of what needed to be done. And the message got through.

Mailboxes are the principal way people thank their postal workers for what they do. One rainy weekend in Almena, Kansas, one of Joseph McFarland's customer's cars got stuck in the mud. The owner abandoned his car by the side of the road and walked home. McFarland found the car while covering his route. He hooked the mired vehicle onto his four-wheel drive jeep and towed it to the owner's house. In gratitude, the farmer bought a new mailbox. "I was glad to have the new box instead of the old roll top [box] that I had been serving," said McFarland, who retired in 1977.

There are times when mailboxes are more important than others. The third of the month is commonly known to postal workers as "Social Security check delivery day." Many carriers have found a common pattern on that day: The mailbox is always accessible, no matter how bad the weather. Back in the 1970s, carrier David Fredley once found a 90-year-old lady busy digging out her mailbox following an 18-inch snowfall on "check day." As he pulled up beside her intending to give her a stern talking-to about the way a woman of her age was going at the snow, the elderly lady beat him to the punch by saying, "I'm shoveling away all this snow so you can put my check in the box." Fredley told her that she had no business doing any such thing at her age and that in the future he would bring her check to her house and hand it to her personally if it ever snowed like that again.

Not all customers are so anxious to get their mail. Instead of digging out the mailbox, one South Dakota resident merely marked the spot where his buried box was supposed to be. It seems that just after a snowplow had cleared the road, "I came to a certain patron's driveway [and] found that the mailbox had been totally covered by the snowplow," reported the carrier. "Then I noticed a small flag on a stick protruding from the snowbank at the road's edge. A few scoops with my snow shovel uncovered the front of the mailbox," the South Dakota carrier remembers.

Carriers are usually quite good about letting their customers know when the mail is there. Besides raising the red signal flag, many carriers, such as Vern Anderson of Edwall, Washington, would honk their car horn. But even this didn't always achieve the desired effect. "I had an insured package for a patron whose box was in front of her house," he said in 1991. "As usual, it was my custom to honk to let her know she was to come out to meet me. On the first honk, a curtain was seen being moved and she peered out. Nothing happened. On the second honk, the same thing. After the third honk, out she came drying her hands on her apron." Her excuse was that she didn't hear the first two times he honked!

On other occasions mailboxes were places to express regrets. Vermont carrier Sharee Brown received this note one wintry morning from an apologetic patron: "Hope it wasn't too inconvenient for you the last two days without the mailbox down there. Kathie and I shoveled snow off the house roof all day long and I was so tired and lame that I just didn't have the energy to dig the mailbox out! Thank you for seeing that we got our mail anyway."

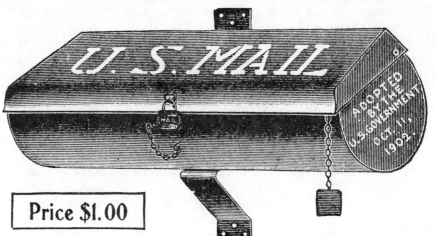
Hessler-approved mailbox ad from 1903.

Another apology came from one of a group of families served by a cluster of boxes. "We are sorry about not having the mailboxes cleaned out for you. I am eight months pregnant and my husband works till 5:00 p.m. No one else seems to care. We really appreciate you delivering despite the mess. We will try to keep it cleaned out for you."

Actually this was a customer's responsibility. Like his colleagues around the country, with each fresh snowfall, Leo Fontaine, a New Hampshire carrier who served from 1968 to 1988, would prepare to hand out a new batch of three-by-five-inch "snow removal notices." "Dear Patrons," the flimsy white paper slips began, "Postal regulations require patrons on rural routes to keep approaches to their mailboxes free of all obstructions including snow. If you are one of those who have customarily kept your box approach clear in the past, we wish to thank you for your cooperation. If you will clear the snow clean all the way to the post and seven or eight feet on either side of (the) post soon after the snow plows have been through it will be greatly appreciated and will not need to be cleared again until the snow plows go through next time. Service may be discontinued temporarily to boxes not properly cleared of snow." A later version of the same type of notice, printed on a full 8-1/2 by 11 inch sheet of paper, gave customers a few options to having ser-

vice suspended if the mailbox could not be cleared of hard-packed snow or frozen ice. These alternatives included using someone else's box that had been cleared, with their permission of course; erecting a temporary mailbox that was accessible to the carrier; meeting the carrier at the snow- or ice-bound box, provided you didn't freeze first; or picking up the mail yourself at the local post office until delivery could be resumed.

Regardless of the season, families often take great pride in their mailboxes. They bear the family name, box number, and sometimes even include the house number. The names can be irksome. Of a 150-box route in the early 1900s, 37 belonged to Andersons, 15 were Smiths and the rest were Jones and Johnsons. Box numbers also have caused problems, although far less frequently. In one instance a carrier got confused because there was a different set of numbers on each side of the same box. The house number, for example, was listed as "12415" on one side and "51421" on the other. The explanation was simple enough. "Well you were coming from the south, so it would be '12415,'" said the home owner. From the north it would be in reverse wouldn't it?

Mailboxes also take the brunt of pent-up hostility. Because of their roadside position, boxes are easy targets for farm machinery, automobiles or teenagers testing their aim with firearms or baseball bats. Youthful pranksters also occasionally frequently take great pride in their ability to crush mailboxes with their four-wheel drive vehicles. One of Russell Graham's South Dakota customers had enough of this sort of mischief. After losing a few mailboxes to pranksters, he mounted one to a solid steel pipe. Sure enough within a matter of days this one was flattened, too. "Only the mailbox won this one," says Graham. "On the ground beside the broken post was the perpetrator's crumpled license plate." Needless to say, later that day the local sheriff made a house call on the kid.

What comes out of a mailbox can frequently be more of a problem than what carriers put in. Much to the embarrassment of a female carrier from Florida, who shall remain nameless, a lizard rocketed out of a box one day, jumping through her open car window and down the front of her blouse. "Normally I am not afraid of lizards, but there is something about one going down your blouse front that makes the difference," she insisted a few years ago. Her immediate reaction was to get at the critter. "By the time I got my blouse half ripped off and the lizard out I was over on the grass," she confessed. Unfortunately, all this took place under the watchful eyes of one of her longtime customers. He thought the show was quite spectacular, especially the part involving the blouse. She still has the vivid memory of how "The old man was about to roll in the street laughing at me."

Retired Kentucky carrier Kenneth Foster is one of the few to ever have come across an "electric mailbox." Each morning he received a bone-rattling shock the minute he touched the box. Because the problem surfaced at the height of a rather muggy summer, he initially thought that it had something to do with static electricity caused by sliding across his car seat, but it was more of a shocking experience than simple static could explain. After putting up with the jolts about as long as he could, he checked the box out with a voltage meter. He discovered that the box was packing a good wallop. Ultimately, in true Sherlock Holmes fashion, he discovered the source of the mystery. It seems that the box, with its metal post, was erected directly over the top of a cross-country high voltage line. In quick order the metal post was replaced with a wooden one and the electrifying problem ceased.

WINNERS AND LOSERS
OF PARCEL POST

Tables can turn. Yesterday's winners can easily become today's losers. History is full of such turnabouts, and parcel post is a good example of how fortunes can change.

Some merchandise could be mailed long before 1913, when parcel post was finally enacted—but not much with any bulk! Legislation passed in 1861 allowed maps, books, cards, seeds and cuttings to be mailable, as long as they didn't weigh more than four pounds. The rate was one cent per ounce on parcels going 1,500 miles or less. The price was doubled on packages going over 1,500 miles. Three years later, another act extended the provisions to include clothing made of wool, cotton, or linen mailed to members of the military. In this case, the rate was eight cents per four ounces. A far more liberal act in 1870 extended the list of mailables to include anything that wasn't considered harmful in itself or to anything else in the mail stream. The postage was one cent per ounce, but again the weight was limited to four pounds, which made freight companies and the railroads ecstatic. This was pathetic, second-rate service.

Postmaster General John Wanamaker advocated the creation of a truly functional parcel post system in the 1890s and like Rural Free Delivery, parcel post was a hard fought battle. It was only a matter of time, he believed. "Nearly every country has established a parcel post, and managed it successfully, to the great satisfaction of the people," he said in one of his annual reports. "The conditions of commerce are much the same all over the world, and if there are no objections from business people in the old countries, after years of experience of the parcel post, there

would not be objections here after it was fairly tried."

Parcel post would be available in other countries long before it was inaugurated here. In 1890, Germany handled over 97 million parcels. Under this service a German farmer could ship dry farm products weighing up to 11 pounds for about one cent a pound. A poultry farmer could mail a goose directly to a consumer living as far as 200 miles or more away for 12 cents. But the same service was not available in the United States.

Wanamaker believed that he recognized the enemy, but was unable to break its death grip. It was left for others to succeed, but for roughly two decades successive postmasters general tried and failed. Others would ultimately succeed, but along the way some of the combatants would briefly become winners, and vice versa by the time parcel post was finally inaugurated in 1913.

Postmaster General John Wanamaker called them "the four insuperable obstacles." They were the giant express companies: Adams Express, American Express, Wells Fargo Express and Southern Express. And, as far as Wanamaker was concerned, they were the four principal reasons why the United States was 30 years behind the rest of the world as far as having an efficient parcel post system. Wanamaker was sure that the nation's postal system could carry parcels at about one-twelfth the cost charged by the shipping companies, but try as he might, he would not get the chance to prove it in the 1890s.

The freight companies cried foul, claiming that they could not fairly compete with the Post Office Department, which had thousands of offices nationwide and an army of clerks and carriers, all paid for by the American people.

Wanamaker's attempts to create an effective parcel post service were blocked at every turn by the lobbying efforts of these four companies and their friends. Writing in the February 1906 issue of *Smith's Magazine*, Charles Cochrane said, "The grip of the express businesses in the United States is so strong that for nearly a third of a century it has thwarted the will of every voter who is not financially interested in the express business." Cochrane called parcel post "A reform [that] is needed," and said that "the public mind should be awakened to the imposition it is suffering through this neglect."

Years dragged on and still "the insuperable four" blocked the way. By 1911, the power of the express companies had become so obvious that *The Independent* proclaimed that "Every child knows that the only hindrance in the way is the rivalry of the express companies."

Others were more specific as to where to place the blame. Senator Thomas Platt was the real culprit, wrote John Brisben Walker in the March 1906 issue of *The Twentieth Century*. "Mr. Platt hedges off all reform in the postal service with as much freedom from concealment as if making a ruling for the United States Express Co., of which he is president," wrote Walker.

Another critic of Platt's, George E. Miller, writing in the August issue of the 1908 *Housekeeper*, dubbed the senator "an insidious, veiled influence." Platt was the choreographer of "Undoubtedly the most skillful, consistent, persistent and successful lobbying ever done in the United States is that by which, over a long series of years, the extension of the American parcel post has been defeated." Miller's opinion was that "For years upon years this lobbying has held a seat in the United States Senate for its leader, in the person of Mr. Platt of New York, and he has there kept patient vigil for the protection of the various express companies of the country."

W.L. Stoddard, writing in *The New Republic*, was more broad in his criticism. Not intent upon tarring any one specific elected official, Stoddard's view was that "The big obstacle that for years stood in the way of an adequate parcel post was Congress, an institution as ill-fitted to debate and decide upon the technical details of transporting mail and bundles as it is to determine railroad freight rates and classifications."

Although the express companies were in the center stage of this turn-of-the-century puppet show, drawing the most scorn, the railroads were to a great extent the hidden puppeteers pulling invisible strings to reinforce their opposition to parcel post. The railroads enjoyed enormous profits from the express business, income that was said to amount to about 50 percent of the gross revenues of the express companies for transporting their freight. The railroads were not opposed to throwing their weight against any thought of a convenient profit-diminishing parcel post system. "An analysis of every movement against the parcel post will invariably trace the inspiration of the movement back to certain railroad directors of large influence in governmental affairs," wrote one commentator in the early 1900s. Alleging that railroads maintained a collusive advantage, it was further charged that "There is not an express company in the country that is not in part owned by directors of the railroads."

As a part of the campaign against parcel post, merchants in crossroads communities were fed a steady diet of gloom and doom by the express companies, tales of how they would be ruined by the mail order houses if parcel post were extended; and, by 1905, they were well on their way to believing what they were being told.

The October 1907 issue of *The Business Magazine* was typical. It tacked the blame squarely on the mail order houses. "The fight for the parcel post system is the fight of the catalogue houses for cheap transportation for its merchandise which it proposes to sell if not by fair means, then by those that are at least questionable and it is not the fight of the farmer."

That need not have been the case if we had emulated other parcel post type systems. In Germany, where there was an effective and well-loved parcel post system, the major mail order houses actually worked hand-in-hand with the nation's little shopkeepers. The wholesale houses furnished slick catalogs to all interested shopkeepers. The catalogs were typically displayed on the stores' counters so that local shoppers could look through them. If they saw anything they liked they could order it directly through their hometown merchant who was someone they knew and trusted. This practice allowed buyers access to a wide array of merchandise— items that in most cases would not be stocked by any small business. One American traveling in Germany was shocked to see how things worked there. "I found myself in the country with my supply of stockings entirely exhausted. I am very partial to a particular make. The village storekeeper had none of that kind, but he at once said: 'I can get them for you in a very short time.' And he did. He posted a letter to Dresden, and by return mail I got the stockings. It was amazing to me, for all my life I have lived in America, where such convenience and good service are unknown," she said in an account published in the May 1911 issue of the *Pictorial Review*. Indeed, no such symbiotic relationship between merchants and consumers existed here at that time.

The enemies of parcel post claimed that a centralized post office-run parcel post system would ruin the country. It would, they asserted, enormously increase the national deficit. That was the exact same type of hysteria that was unleashed in the fight against R.F.D., and once again the monster was proven to have no real teeth. The passage of time disproved the thought that R.F.D. would bankrupt the country; actually, its existence was largely responsible for lowering postal deficits. Writing in 1907, Postmaster General George Von L. Meyer observed that the deficit in 1896 was $11.5 million. A decade later it had shrunk to $6.7 million, despite the expenses associated with launching rural delivery, which by then cost $27 million. Von L. Meyer also saw parcel post as a way of further improving the postal service's overall profit picture.

In the war of words over parcel post service *The National Hardware Bulletin* and the *Dry Goods Economist*, as might be expected, took strong editorial stands against the idea. Such opponents typically tied their stance to the shrinking size of rural America. Why should America waste money serving a smaller and smaller part of its people, they argued? After all, they asserted, farms are being abandoned at an alarming rate, youths were fleeing the family farms in droves and, just for good measure, they added that "the country churches were dead." So why waste money on the backwoods?

Other publications forecast a bleak future if parcel post legislation passed. In true domino fashion, the March 1911 edition of *Hardware Dealers' Magazine* predicted that if you "Take away the local market and values fall; the town or village merchants go out of business; stores are closed, [and] there is no further need for the building of business blocks; grass grows in the streets, except in front of the local post office—and the farmers do not even need to visit that, when the rural free delivery system is provided." The demise of small retailers and merchants was seen as the first step in the collapse of this all-important economic food chain.

Jobbers were also expected to be hurt. That made sense. Anytime that the consumer and the producer are brought closer together, the middlemen get hurt. But arguably that is the way things go. The jobber's business was created because the retail market was remote from the source of supply.

When distance no longer is a factor, the importance of the jobber ceases to be as crucial as it once may have been.

Charles W. Burrows, the president of the National One Cent Postage Association, went even further, spreading the net to include newspapers. "With the disappearance of the local merchant, must go the local newspaper," he wrote in a 1911 article titled "Against Parcel Post." Burrows believed that manufacturers would subsequently be hurt, too. Once the mail order houses got big enough to really corner the market, they would manufacture their own goods, he predicted. It was feared that this would result in the creation of enormous mail order trusts that would drain the incomes of the rural communities and aggravate the evils of centralized wealth.

A more simplistic view was that "The rural village, now the center of social life, will disappear. There will be nothing left at the railroad station except a post office and a pair of big scales."

Advocates for parcel post—including the Farmer's Union, Farmer's National Congress, National Grange, American Florists Association, and Postal Progress League—quickly refuted such claims. They observed that there was a growing "back to the country" movement by the early 1910s; that youths would certainly enjoy farm life better if they could buy things by mail; and, as for the country church issue, "they were killed off 70 years earlier." On the contrary, "Never was country life more progressive, better organized or more lifeful and hopeful," stated *The Independent* in January 1911. "We are not worried at all when we contemplate a picture involving a more substantial country home, with its isolation abolished, hidden among the hills, but visited daily by the rural free delivery carrier, even [though] he shall have in his automobile a ten-pound package for the housewife," the paper emphasized.

"Back to the farm" was more than a mere slogan. It was an effort to recapture the values of our agricultural past, a rekindling of what in 1912 Mississippi Congressman Ezekiel Chandler, Jr., called "the conviction that agriculture is the foundation rock of the country's prosperity."

At the time of its founding, America was overwhelmingly an agricultural nation. When our first census was taken in 1790, over nine-tenths of the population lived off the land or in rural America. This majority began to steadily erode, dropping to about 60 percent by the start of the Civil War. The decline in the rural population continued following the war. But, since the fourth quarter of the 19th century the mid-section of the country was no longer an area to be crossed as quickly as possible on one's way west. With the completion of the transcontinental railroads, the heartlands were becoming places of growth and prosperity. However, this was more a part of inland migration by immigrants and city dwellers. The fact of the matter was that there weren't many unproductive farm sites in the east. The Governor of New York, for one, said that he had "No idea where such deserted farms were in New York State." The notion that there was available land in his state was a myth. But there was land in the territories.

At its core the United States might have been an agricultural nation but unfortunately, territorial homesteaders had little real power. Although many of those who founded the republic were farmers, few farmers were members of Congress in the second half of the 19th century. This omission was noticeable, so much so that President James Polk lamented in 1846 that farmers "have heretofore not ... received the bounties or favors of Government."

Other groups were far more fortunate. City dwellers were politically harder to ignore. City political figures could deliver large blocks of votes at election times, and the concentrated party structures were capable of wielding great influence. Cities were focal points of political power.

By contrast, rural America was comprised of scattered hamlets with little power base. The Homestead Act, signed into law in 1862, provided land to those willing to farm and improve the property over a specific period. Urban poor and new immigrants were seen as the largest beneficiaries of this act. Unfortunately, the nobility of the Homestead Act was swiftly eclipsed by its accompanying greed and graft. Land speculators and outright crooks managed to divert over 80 percent of all acreage to self serving purposes, upping the cost of the land from free title to wildly inflated prices.

The railroads were also keen to capitalize on their share of the government's largess. They had received immense tracts of land, amounting to about 150 million acres, as track right of ways. These lands were valuable incentives for track laying. The railroads made money from the sale of lands given to them free by the government. Their tracks also made money by moving settlers west and farm products east. They and their partners, the express companies, didn't want Uncle Sam taking any share of the profits.

In the battle for parcel post neither side was totally playing fair. Both pro and con forces homed in on all sorts of horror stories to support their point of view. The pro-parcel post camp reported story after story of how helpless farmers were losing their shirts to outrageous profiteering by the railroads and the shipping companies. *Collier's Weekly* presented a tale of exorbitant rates being charged to one New York farmer. "I shipped thirty-six baskets of peaches by the American Express Company," the grower stated. "The peaches sold for thirty cents a basket, making a total of ten dollars and eight cents. The express charges were ten dollars and four cents, and the money order for remittal cost three cents. The total proceeds of the thirty-six baskets were thus seventy-three cents. It cost me, however, fifteen cents a basket to pick and pack the fruit, or five dollars and forty cents in all. I thus suffered a net loss on the shipment of four dollars and sixty-seven cents," the farmer claimed.

Another publication, the *American Agriculturist*, published a similar tale. This time the product was cauliflower and the losses amounted to $1.10 on a shipment of 27 crates.

The express companies ate the profits because the farmers were over the barrel. They either had to ship their perishable products or let them rot. At the same time shipping firms were doing a bumper crop of business. In one year alone Adams Express handled over 67 million transactions. Another of "the insuperable four" shipped nearly a quarter of a million packages between the east and west coasts during that same period. Such shipments were a boon to their business, but that business cost American consumers dearly.

The big four freight companies were indeed profiting handsomely on their monopoly. Rates varied according to destinations, but from New York City to Atlanta, Georgia, a 100-pound package cost $4 to be handled by American Express. The rates to more inaccessible parts of the country commanded a higher premium, amounting to as much as $20 per 100 pounds.

Farmers had R.F.D., but the express companies had the farmers by the nose when it came to shipping anything heavy. It was as if, wrote Lewis Edwin Theiss in 1911, "the rural free delivery is a bird with its wings clipped—it carries only those things that can be put in a four-pound package, and it carries them at prohibitive cost." Compared to some contemporary European parcel post rates, ours were high: 16 cents per pound. More routinely, where Uncle Sam charged 64 cents to transport four pounds, in Germany the cost was 30 cents for 110 pounds of the same stuff.

In all fairness, Germany wasn't exactly a comparable country to match with the United States. On average, German parcels traveled about 40 miles to their destination. American parcels were averaging 540 miles. Besides, Germany owned its railway system and it did not make its postal system pay for transporting mail. By the 1910s, German parcel post volume had grown by two-thirds in about 20 years, jumping to over 300 million parcels.

The parcel post systems in European countries were an ideal way of showing how bad off American's had it. Our four pound limit was minute compared to the European nations. Switzerland had no constraints whatsoever, Belgium had a maximum weight limit of 132 pounds for parcels, Germany and Austria had 110 pound ceilings, France's maximum was 22 pounds, and Great Britain, Italy and the Netherlands had 11 pound limits.

Pricewise, American mailers got no bargain either. An 11-pound package that cost the equivalent of 10 cents to mail in the Netherlands, 12 cents in Austria, 13 cents in Germany, 16 cents in France and Belgium, 20 cents in Italy and 22 cents in Great Britain, in the United States cost $1.76, but you had to mail that in three separate packages to comply with the four pound limit.

Although he had left office, former Postmaster General George Von L. Meyer continued to speak out loudly on behalf of the farmers' need for free mail delivery and parcel post. "The isolation in many parts of the country has been overcome; people are in daily communication with their friends and the rest of the world; daily papers and magazines are delivered to every door on the rural routes, and enlightenment and information are being spread. Medical men say that already the establishment of the rural delivery is having its effect on the mentality of the country dwellers, and that because of it there is even now a decrease in insanity," he said; but, another important ingredient in the recipe for the well-being of the rural patrons—parcel post—was still sorely missing.

Oddly, of all of the factors being considered in the fight for parcel post, little notice was taken of the welfare of rural women and the curative powers of parcel post on the quality of their lives. Farm women tended to live isolated lives, with no easy means of communications. Life was hard. There were few conveniences and far fewer educational and cultural opportunities for them. And, while their husbands occasionally could disappear into town on some errand or another, farm wives more often than not stayed at home immersed in the endless workload around the farm. It was little wonder that so many rural women wound up in asylums, but still few in the parcel post movement concentrated on the many ways parcel post might be of use to women. The Woman's Suffrage Movement would help change some aspects of women's rights, but it didn't help here.

Between 1910 and 1912, the political climate was beginning to change. For one thing the American public was beginning to catch on to the fact that some of the express companies were handling parcels for foreign post offices at a rate of as little as 24 cents each. It didn't matter where in the United States these parcels were going. According to the shipping companies, they could make a profit at that rate. On the other hand, American shippers were paying anywhere from 25 cents to $23 for almost the exact same service. Clearly the express companies were doing some heavy-duty price gouging. Then too, the American people were beginning to take notice that 43 other countries had economical and reliable parcel post services. Americans were beginning to wonder what did they know that we didn't.

And Congress was getting the message. The 1910 elections ushered in many freshmen members of Congress who recognized that the American people wanted parcel post. Some of the senior members of Congress reluctantly recognized the necessity of the nationwide parcel posts system, too. "If we don't enact this legislation," stated one Republican congressman, "the next Congress will. We had better give them something and get the credit for it."

By 1912, the grip of the express companies also began to loosen as six brand-new freight companies emerged in addition to the four original freight companies that plagued Wanamaker. The fact that there were more freight companies to fight was not a cause for concern, largely because the group had by then been placed under the jurisdiction of the Interstate Commerce Commission as a result of the Hepburn Rate Law of 1906.

The express companies soon found themselves in hot water with the Commission. Allegations of charging "unjust, unreasonable and extortionate rates" were brought against each of the companies. The accusations brought by the New York Merchants' Association and several hundred other business groups also included claims of over billings and double billings. The Commission's investigation showed that there was a pattern of abuses, particularly billing both the sender and recipient for the same shipment and overcharging on insurance and handling. The winds of time gradually wore down on the express companies whose scandalous business practices diminished their influence on Capitol Hill.

Congress responded by churning out more than a dozen bills relating to parcel post. New York Congressman William Sulzer introduced legislation that was simple, and long overdue: "In this country the citizen owns the post office and wants to use it as his transportation company. Its end is to keep him informed; to make known to the people his wishes; to provide means by which he may communicate with his fellow citizens for their mutual benefit; and to supply his wants and dispose of his wares at the least possible cost, in the shortest possible time, and with the greatest possible security." Sulzer's position was that "The time is at hand for Congress to heed the insistent demand of the people for an extended parcel post along the lines of my bill—the express companies to the contrary, notwithstanding."

Sulzer's bill was backed by all of the advocates of postal reform. It proposed increasing the weight of domestically mailed packages from four to eleven pounds in keeping with the guidelines of the Universal Postal Union, the international body that negotiated the exchange of mail worldwide and limiting the applicable rates to eight cents per pound. The United States was one of the founders of this organization.

Although the United States led in the creation of this international body, when it came to parcel post, it was like a backwater nation. While many countries at that time allowed parcels of 11 pounds or more to be transported by mail, the United States had an unreasonably low four-pound limit.

Opponents of Sulzer's bill objected to any extension of the domestic transportation of merchandise beyond the present four-pound limit. This ceiling made little sense and the strict adherence to it was dubbed "childish, as well as illogical."

This imbalance forced some foreign postal administrations to make special arrangements when it came to handling parcels mailed to the United States. As part of its service, the Imperial German postal system maintained a "Parcel Agency" in New York City and Brooklyn, as well as in Jersey City, New Jersey. This service was provided for the benefit of German manufacturers, shippers and merchants that did business in the United States. In the 1890s and early 1900s, bright blue German postal wagons were used in this country to deliver packages weighing up to the Universal Postal Union's 11-pound limit.

Postmaster General Frank Hitchcock had studied the German parcel post system. He longed to start a similar system here. "I first became interested in the subject of the Parcel Post while abroad," he once said when asked how he happened to champion such a service in this country. "I have made several trips to Europe since to investigate the matter. I saw the system in operation there and the great advantage it afforded the people. Then I decided we should adopt it here."

By 1912, the time to make good on Hitchcock's plan was at hand. According to Oregon Senator Jonathan Bourne, Jr., "The subject has been discussed far and wide for many years. Every argument that could be advanced for or against has been repeated time and again. Labor organizations, granges, farmers' unions, merchants, associations and many commercial organizations have considered the subject and adopted resolutions setting forth their views and desires .... After this extended consideration had been had, there could be no doubt that a large majority of the people of the United States should establish a parcel post service." The only question remaining, said Bourne was not whether such a system is established, but how that service should work.

The time was ripe for at attempting a limited parcel post system, one particularly targeted towards rural communities. This was a subtle tactic. By going after the people that were least likely to be served cheaply by the express companies first, the rest of the nation could fall into place as soon as the benefits were seen.

Postmaster General Frank Hitchcock asked Congress for just such a limited scheme, seeking permission to deliver packages weighing up to 11 pounds to rural residents. At the same time Hitchcock asked for an appropriation to investigate a general parcel post. This was a carefully crafted first step under which the death grip of the express companies and railroads would be broken.

Hitchcock made no bones about what he planned to do, if given half a chance. Late in 1911, he advised the Senate Committee on Post Offices and Post Roads:

> *I favor making a beginning on the rural routes, but that beginning should be followed as rapidly as possible with an extension of the parcel post system to other branches of the postal system. My plan was to start with the rural routes, follow that almost immediately with delivery in the carrier service in cities and towns, and after those two branches of the service are organized, to take over the railway express business, thus making a general system.*

This was straightforward enough. Unfortunately, some supporters such as *The American Journal of Clinical Medicine* saw his approach as a halfway measure; but, it told its readers, "for all that [it] may be like the proverbial 'half loaf.'" The position of the medical journal was that "The physician's interest is that of the people as a whole. His prosperity depends upon their prosperity. Certainly, he should lend all his influence to making the parcel post a reality and of widest utility."

Finally, with the backing of Senator Jonathan Bourne of Oregon, Postmaster General Hitchcock got the chance his predecessors had only dreamed of getting. Congress appropriated $750,000 for the initiation of the long-awaited parcel post system, scheduled to be put into operation on January 1, 1913. For Hitchcock, one of the best things about the service was its immense convenience for rural families. For them it would be an important extension of Rural Free Delivery, which by 1913 was a thriving postal operation.

Star Route contractors were one of the first to suffer from the introduction of parcel post. In many cases these contractors transported mail as well as freight and this profitable sideline was curtailed with the onset of parcel post. Some contractors bailed out almost immediately. Within two weeks of the introduction of parcel post, the Kellogg Stage Co. in Oregon threw in the towel on its four mail routes, deciding to abandon mail service in the central portion of the state rather than be forced to haul postal parcels.

Another irate Star Route contractor, F.T. Deason, blamed Congress for the damage. He voiced his displeasure to his Congressman, Thomas W. Hardwick, saying:

> I set myself with pen in hand to write you a few lines to let you know that you have played the devil with me. I am the mail [contractor] from McIntyre to Irvington [Georgia] and took the contract to carry the mail three times a day, distance three-and-one-third miles, for $319 a year .... You fixed the law so I could not [drink on the job] and now you have fixed up a thing called the possum post [parcel post] .... When I made this contract I could carry the mail in a road cart and a Texas pony, and haul [freight] on the side; now the [freight] has struck and this post business has swelled so I have to get a mule and wagon. Now, when I made this [deal] to carry the mail, I did not know anything about this darn foolishness of sending livestock and farm implements the mail [by parcel post]. I thought that this was just campaign talk and had no idea the Congress would be fool enough to pass any such law. I ain't no man to quit his job and I

> never got my bondsmen in trouble, but I'll tell you this thing is getting serious and I want help .... You have just about ruined [my freight business] and you have worse than ruined me.

Rural carriers also suffered. The loads far exceeded official expectations, although the carriers had inklings of what was to come.

Most envisioned the worst. "I am expecting something like a rush with parcel post," predicted Calvin E. Serong, a rural carrier from Mead, Washington. In December 1912, Serong confessed that "I have not decided yet whether I'll get four horses and a moving van or a three-ton auto truck (to handle the load)."

T.S. Burch of Missouri, who used a motorcycle for his 26-mile mail route, couldn't bear the thought of giving up his two-wheeler. He told his cohorts "I rather think I will devise some plan to carry the butter, eggs, potatoes in a left-handle bag, tie the chickens, ducks and geese on the right handle, and put the goats and pigs in a (sidecar)."

Jake Neversweat had other visions. The New Hampshire carrier knew of a colleague who was laid up when his horse got frightened by a truck and ran off into a ditch. Everything was a jumble in the December 1912 accident. Carrier, horse, wagon and the mail were all mixed into one common heap. Neversweat imagined that it was one year later and the same accident just happened. Everything was the same, except now parcels were a part of the injured carrier's load. "Beside 856 pieces of mail, he had, as parcel post, seven dozens of eggs, two 10-pound sacks of buck wheat flour, four pounds of butter, and one can of maple syrup, a gallon jug full of butter milk, two cakes of limburger and three quarts of sour kraut. "The carrier dreamed that his wagon caught fire, that he fished out his parcel post stuff, baked it into buck wheat cakes, made himself a corn fodder tent and lived happily ever afterwards."

Contrary to such whimsical notions, on the eve of the start of the service one of the common fallacies was that rural carriers could handle parcel post if it was given a try. The Louisville Courier-Journal echoed this common misconception by claiming that "the rural carriers already have sufficient equipment for carrying the packages." However, the opposite was true. Rural carriers were totally unprepared for the avalanche of mail that was to come.

ODD THAT IT CAME BY MAIL

Initially, Parcel Post regulations were broadly interpreted, but as more bizarre, unwieldy and perishable items were shipped, new regulations had to be adopted to protect the carriers, as well as the products.

Everyone likes to be the first at something, and the introduction of a general parcel post system on January 1, 1913, afforded an opportunity for many individuals and towns to share in the novelty. Of course some parcel post "firsts" were more notable than others. Postmaster General Frank H. Hitchcock is credited with officially mailing the nation's first parcel post package from the Washington, D.C., post office shortly after midnight. It was a small silver cup inscribed to the postmaster of New York City.

Edward M. Morgan, the New York City postmaster, reciprocated by mailing a much taller silver cup to his boss, Frank Hitchcock, at precisely the same time. This trophy, the first to be mailed from New York City, was furnished by former Postmaster General John Wanamaker, who initially proposed such a domestic parcel system during his tenure. There was more to the fact that Morgan's cup was taller than Hitchcock's than mere coincidence. It was a symbolic political slap at Hitchcock. The Wanamaker/Morgan and the Hitchcock cups are in the Smithsonian's collection and are on display at the National Postal Museum.

While these cups represent the first objects officially mailed under the parcel post scheme, the first package to be delivered reportedly went to the New Jersey home of President-elect Woodrow Wilson on January 1, 1913. The Woodrow Wilson Club of Princeton mailed an 11-pound package of apples at a local post office at precisely 12:01 a.m., when the system was inaugurated. By a previous arrangement, the carrier assigned to normally deliver Governor Wilson's mail, David Gransom, received the parcel even before the canceling ink was dry on the stamps and reportedly delivered it by 12:04 a.m. Wilson, who was keeping a New Year's Eve vigil, is said to have met Gransom at the door, signed for the package, and presented the carrier with the pencil.

On the first day of parcel post service prominent people were mailing parcels all over the place. Former Postmaster General John Wanamaker mailed a set of 48 engraved spoons to President Taft. The first parcel post shipment from Chicago was a package sent by the *Record-Herald* to Sumner Curtis, the newspaper's Washington correspondent.

In short order Chicagoans found many interesting uses for parcel post. Within a matter of days, one Chicago restaurant began sending business leaders their lunches by mail. The 300 meals to bankers, brokers, and real estate agents were delivered in pasteboard packages. Initially tried as an experiment, the lunch-by-mail scheme proved highly successful.

The growth of parcel post was phenomenal. Forty million packages were handled in January 1913, and fifty million more came through the postal system the following month. During the first six months of operation approximately 300 million parcels were handled.

As a swan song, Postmaster General Frank Hitchcock, who left office on March 4, 1913, added

Special Delivery service to parcel post, effective March 1 of that year. Under Hitchcock's order, Special Delivery was available for 10 cents.

The introduction of Collect-on-Delivery Service on July 1, 1913, only added to the popularity of parcel post. The popularity further grew when postal officials increased the allowable weight of parcels. In 1913, the maximum weight was increased from 11 to 20 pounds for the first and second zones. A short time later the maximum rose again, from 20 to 50 pounds.

With the introduction of parcel post, rural mail carriers covered more than a million miles providing service where no private express companies operated. Prior to that, farmers had to take their produce to the nearest town large enough to support a freight office, which added to the price of transporting their goods. But with the combination of R.F.D. and Parcel Post, package service was available right at their mailbox.

The deluge of parcel post mail was bad enough, but things got worse with bad weather. F.J. Elliott, the postmaster of Bend, Oregon, filed a report to postal officials explaining the delay of mail to residents, just like he was supposed to, only the explanation of what he planned to do about it was a bit odd. He told officials, "Due to eight inches of snow and non-delivery on Sunday, we had 300 Parcel Post packages on hand Monday night." Under the "Action Taken" section of the report, Elliott wrote "We cussed the weather and delivered them Tuesday."

By far one of the largest objects ever moved through parcel post was a bank. Not all at once, of course, but practically brick by brick. When W.H. Coltharp, in charge of building the Bank of Vernal, California, was confronted with the task of getting bricks for the bank, he turned to parcel post. The bricks that Coltharp wanted were produced by the Salt Lake Pressed Brick Co., located 427 miles from Vernal. Instead of paying four times the cost of shipping them by freight, Coltharp arranged for the bricks to be shipped in 50 pound packages. Needless to say, the Salt Lake City and Vernal postmasters, as well as the Uintah Railroad, all responsible for hauling the bricks, became frantic as tons of bricks piled up. Memos flew between the postmasters and finally to Postmaster General Albert Burleson. Although it was too late to stem the tide of bricks, which threatened to overwhelm the tiny Vernal post office, Burleson and his staff rewrote the defective regulation to limit to 200 pounds the total weight of parcel post that one consignor could send to one consignee in a day. In a letter announcing the amendment to the regulation, Burleson noted

that "it is not the intent of the United States Postal Service that buildings be shipped through the mail." The residents got around this by each becoming a recipient, accepting small packets of brick that they personally delivered to the building site. In the end, all 40 tons of bricks were delivered for Coltharp's two-story bank.

By the "Roaring Twenties," parcel post had become firmly established, and in subsequent decades it would prove to be an important facet of American life, especially in the rural communities and remote areas where travel to the city for merchandise was limited.

Many things entered the mail stream when parcel post service started, and not all of them were pleasant. A near riot erupted at the Nashville post office when a can of fertilizer burst open. According to one account, because of the smell, "There was a near-mutiny among the office force who were handling the packages."

In all likelihood, Anne Olson was probably the first to "move" by mail. Her household was sent by parcel post. Postal officials were flabbergasted when she showed up at the Seattle post office with her belongings in tow. Her stove was among the largest of the articles to be mailed. It was packed in a hefty barrel. She wanted sufficient stamps to cover the postage for sending her household goods from Seattle to Quinault, Washington. Mrs. Olson's novel idea was about one-quarter as expensive as the cost of shipping by freight.

Over the years, children have also found their way into the mail stream. When parcel post was introduced in 1913 a great many questions arose about what specifically could or could not be mailed. Immigration officials in New York City had no other way of getting an eight-year-old Bavarian girl to her father ... so they mailed her in 1913. The child arrived at the New Lexington, Ohio, post office was explained by this note: "This child, Julia Kohan, is going to her father, Box 117 RFD No. 4, Lexington, Ohio." The local postmaster gave the waif a hearty breakfast before handing her over to a rural carrier for final delivery. In this case, the postmaster on the receiving end had no choice in the matter, but early in 1914 the postmaster of Stratford, Oklahoma, G.W. Merrill, wrote to postal service headquarters for a ruling on the following: "J.B. Denton, of this place, asks if he can have a child, two years of age, sent by parcel post from Twin Falls, Idaho, to this place. Finding nothing in the parcel post regulations covering such a case, I am referring him to the Department." Needless to say, Merrill's letter caused a mild sensation when it reached the attention of Second Assistant Postmaster General Joseph Stewart. After making a hurried review of the regulations himself, Stewart concluded that Merrill was right. Nothing specifically covered the mailing of human beings, when considered as a distinct category from other living things. At that point, Stewart ruled that all living things, including children, were barred from the mails. The only exception he said were queen bees. While Stewart's ruling would not hold up for long, the ban on kids would remain.

(Today postal regulations allow for a variety of warm- and cold-blooded critters to be carried by mail. Among the permissible cold-blooded creatures are baby alligators, turtles, frogs, goldfish, bees, crickets, ladybugs, praying mantises and lizards; while warm-blooded mail can include chicks and ducklings.)

Unlike the postmaster at Stratford, Oklahoma, many other local postmasters acted without asking for guidance. According to one account, published in *The Postmasters' Advocate*, a young cherub was entrusted to the mail by its mother in 1914. The child traveled from Stillwell, Indiana, to South Bend. It seems that the parents had been involved in a rather nasty divorce proceeding and when the father had instituted action to acquire custody of the child, who was then only a few months old, the mother moved to Stillwell. When the court awarded custody to the father, the mother complied with the decree. She reportedly sent the child in a safe container marked "Live Baby" and mailed it to the father for 17 cents. The baby was tenderly handled by postal workers and was delivered safe and sound.

May Pierstroff was another precious package that was sent via parcel post. The four-year-old blond was mailed from Grangeville, Idaho, to her grandparents in Lewiston, Idaho, on February 19, 1914. This time the total charge, calculated on the basis of mailing chickens, was 53 cents. This fee reflected her weight—48-1/2 pounds—which was just 1-1/2 pounds shy of the 50-pound chicken limit. May, the daughter of Mr. and Mrs. John E. Pierstroff, was packed off in care of "Uncle Sam" because the postage was cheaper than train fare. The local newspaper, *The Lewiston Tribune*, reported the event, in part, this way: "Harry Morris, conductor on the Camas Prairie train between Grangeville and Lewiston was surprised on entering the mail car to collect (the) fare from the little passenger, (instead only) to be shown the parcel post stamps at-

tached (on a tag) to her coat. Morris retreated and the child occupied the mail car during the trip. She was delivered to the home of her grandmother, Mrs. Vennigerholz, by mail clerk Leonard Mochel."

Despite the pleas and demands of postal officials, children continued to be mailed. Six-year-old Edna Neff was mailed from Pensacola, Florida, to Christiansburg, Virginia, in 1915. The child's parents were separated and her mother had fallen on hard times. A Florida probation officer, who temporarily had custody of the youngster, could not afford the train fare for the child and an adult traveling companion, consequently the child was "mailed." According to a contemporary newspaper account, the cost of sending Edna to her father in Virginia was 15 cents.

Transporting children through the mail wasn't always pleasant. The handling of "Parcella Post" was possibly the oddest and saddest case of a child sent by mail. "Parcella Post" is the anonymous name placed on a headstone. The rest of the inscription reads: "An infant whose unknown parents sent the little body by mail to an Albany (New York) undertaker Nov. 20, 1922. Buried here through the kindness of individuals Nov. 27, 1922." In this case postal workers didn't know that a child was in the package mailed to the undertakers.

Marmi Hood, age 5, and Evan Hedge, 4, were also "mailed." They were sent by mail to their fathers who had voluntarily remained inside the plant to care for idled machinery during a strike at the Aluminum Company of America plant in Alco, Tennessee. The children received safe conduct past the picketers and were delivered to their fathers at a rate of $2.26 each. After a two-hour stay, the sobbing children were mailed back home. They were picked up by a carrier at the plant office, driven back to the Alco post office, and returned to their mothers by "special delivery."

Despite the official ban on mailing children, kids were considered special. In 1921, Postmaster General Will H. Hayes attempted to humanize the postal system following the Burleson years by allowing children to be weighed by postal employees. Working in conjunction with the U.S. Public Health Service, parcel post truck drivers were authorized to weigh infants using the scales on their vehicles. This practice allowed mothers to keep track of the progress of their childrens' growth. This modest effort was extremely well-received.

SCANDALOUS GROWING PAINS FOR R.F.D.

"No crime calls for sterner reprobation than the crime of the corruptionist in public life and of the man who seeks to corrupt him. The bribe-taker and the bribe-giver are equally guilty."

President Theodore Roosevelt, 1903

Between 1896 and 1906 rural home delivery became an established reality for more and more Americans. There were 1,259 R.F.D. routes by 1900, 8,298 by 1902, 24,566 by 1904, and 35,767 by 1906. Such rapid growth provided ample opportunities for graft and corruption, the worst of which occurred while Augustus Caesar Machen was the General Superintendent of the Free Delivery Service.

Machen's actions fit Oscar Wilde's line in Chapter 2 of *Picture of Dorian Gray* to a tee: "The only way to get rid of a temptation is to yield to it." Machen succumbed ihn the worst way. The Free Delivery Service, which included city as well as rural mail delivery services, was a garden full of plums ripe for the plucking. Augustus Machen was a greedy picker. Machen made all kinds of deals with contractors and confederates, which wound up being worth tens-of-thousands of dollars. He was apparently into almost anything. He took bribes and kickbacks on an array of expendables, such as twine used to wrap packages, rubber bands, ink for writing pens, and handstamp ink pads for postmarking devices. And, he also was up to his elbows in influencing the lucrative purchases of postal service equipment, such as check writing machines, canceling machines and postal scales.

What's worse, Machen wasn't alone. Others were charged with their involvement in schemes of their own, including George Beavers, who supervised the salary and allowances section of the postal system, and James Tyner, Assistant U.S. Attorney General

for the Post Office. In short order Beavers resigned and Tyner was dismissed. Forced to ultimately stand trial on charges of conspiring to defraud the government, Tyner was acquitted of wrongdoing. Beavers, who was said to have used "every pull and influence possible" to avoid prosecution, plead guilty in 1906 to defrauding the government in connection with time recording devices. He was sentenced to two years in the penitentiary at Moundsville, West Virginia.

Machen was removed from office as the head of the Free Delivery Service on a charge of malfeasance. But being sacked was only the beginning. He also was quickly arrested on charges of receiving bribes in connection with a contract for fasteners used to secure mailboxes onto lampposts. This contract would prove to be his undoing, one that led to a nasty labyrinth of other improprieties. Investigators found ample evidence that the postal system purchased about $140,000 worth of the fasteners over a 10-year period, with Machen receiving at least $22,000 of the amount paid to the contractors during his tenure as the head of his department. The fasteners, produced by Samuel A. Groff, a police officer in Washington, D.C., were not acquired under any sort of competitive bid process as required by standard operating procedures.

The odd thing is that the Groff fastener was actually a good device. It should have been selected for use based upon its merits alone, but the inventor wanted to ensure its acceptance by greasing Machen's palm. The fastener consisted of two interlocking iron cleats, one bolted to the mailbox, the other to the post. The cleats were joined by sliding one over the other in a grooved socket. The mated cleats were fastened securely by a locking spring. This style of fastener was basically used until the mid-1950s.

An army of postal inspectors began searching for other dirty dealings involving Machen, among others, and they swiftly hit pay dirt. The magnitude of the crimes was shocking. The only other time that the Post Office Department was rocked so severely by such scandal was in 1881 when Second Assistant Postmaster General Thomas J. Brady and Stephen W. Dorsey, secretary to the Republican National Committee, went to trial on charges of rigging mail transportation contracts. (In a twist of irony, this 19th century trial was played out in the same courtroom where Machen ultimately would be forced to defend himself.)

By mid-summer 1903, President Theodore Roosevelt made it clear that everyone associated with such wrongdoing was going to be prosecuted. He ordered government investigators "not only to take up the cases in which indictments have been found or hereafter may be found, but to examine all charges that have been made against officials in the Postal Service, with the view to the removal and prosecution of all guilty men in the service, and the prosecution of guilty men whether in the service or not."

Machen was the central figure throughout the investigations. He joined the Post Office Department as political appointee during the Democratic administration of Grover Cleveland, but switched parties when the Republicans later won the White House. Considered "dead broke" when appointed, Machen soon acquired considerable wealth. He always claimed that it came from betting on horses.

Throughout 1903 and 1904, Machen was not depicted as a sympathetic figure. He was characterized as a political chameleon and an opportunist. His physical appearance wasn't ignored by the press, either. One 1904 publication wrote, "Machen has an interesting face. His florid complexion, massive neck, and strong, wide shoulders, suggest the butcher which Machen was in Toledo in the (1880s)." He also was said to possess "the shrewd smile of the capitalist and promoter," as well as "the heavy eyebrows, slight gray mustache, flashing brown eyes and intellectual forehead of the business man." His posture in court, slouching back in his chair with his legs outstretched and his hands clasped in front of his ample waist, appeared in

many cartoons of the time. Illustrators also did not fail to notice his fondness for large diamonds which adorned his hands and shirt front, a fact that helped to portray him as a sporting man.

Shortly after Machen was indicted two of his closest assistants were also fired and arrested on charges that they defrauded the government in connection with the purchase of leather pouches for rural carriers. The clerks—C. Ellsworth Upton and Thomas W. McGregor—were accused of working with a mailbag manufacturer to inflate the price of bags from 60 cents to 90 cents each, with the understanding that 40 percent of the price would go to them in exchange for a large government contract. Actually, the pouches were produced by another firm at a cost of about 35 cents each, resulting in greater profits for the alleged conspirators. By the summer of 1903, news accounts of the arrests of Upton and McGregor were expressing the hope that "This may be the beginning—the entering wedge into the tens of thousands that have been dumped into the Rural Free Delivery hopper." And it was!

Other schemes involved awarding an unnecessary and wildly inflated contract to paint curbside mailboxes, sometimes as frequently as once each year. Machen and his colleagues went even farther than that by authorizing the contractor to paint new mailboxes at the factory where they were produced. The manufacturer's contract called for the production of painted boxes. This meant that two firms were being paid to paint the same identical mailboxes, with Machen sharing in the overpayment. Another rip-off focused on inflating the prices paid for shoulder straps used for rural mail satchels.

Within the year, 17 postal officials hastily resigned or were fired and 44 indictments were issued against 31 individuals, 10 of whom were senior postal employees, one of which was Machen. According to the government's principal investigator, Joseph Bristow, the graft-takers and crooks netted as much as $300,000 to $400,000.

Eugene D. Scheble was one of the outsiders that was charged. A dentist from Toledo, Ohio, Scheble developed an inferior style of lamppost letter box and then, apparently for a price, convinced Machen of its merits. Ultimately nearly 50,000 of this style of mailbox were purchased before the conspiracy was revealed. In this case, local postmasters were among the first to smell a rat. Letter boxes galore were shipped to countless crossroads post offices with instructions to the local postmasters to place them wherever they wanted them. Many of these same postmasters soon complained to Washington that they were being inundated with unwanted letter boxes. They were so numerous that boxes sometimes were placed on trees and fence posts only a short distance from one another along countless rural roads just to get rid of them. This was a waste since in reality a farm family's R.F.D. box was just as good a repository for mailing a letter as was the government's boxes.

These lamppost style boxes were intended for letter mail only. Packages or periodicals could not be conveniently mailed in such letter boxes, as the slot for depositing mail was relatively small. To accommodate parcels, the Post Office Department contracted for another type of box, known as "package boxes" in 1893. These were placed alongside the letter boxes.

According to postal archives, initially it was hoped that the larger package boxes could be suspended from the same lampposts as their companion letter boxes, but because of their size, the idea was dropped.

Machen got his fingers dirty in the package box contract, too. The initial 1893 contract for producing the big boxes was awarded to William H. Spencer, but in fact, the actual contractor was Isaac McGiehan. Spencer merely served as a "dummy" corporation head. Four years later when the contract was rebid, McGiehan again won the award, this time under the name of the Columbian Manufacturing Co. He won the contract again in 1901, only this time he received the award under the name of the Columbia Supply Co. Actually, investigators found that none of these firms produced anything. In reality, all of the boxes were produced by a sub-contractor, the Van Dorn Iron Works of Cleveland, Ohio, a firm whose principal line of work was fabricating jail cells.

Postal inspectors established a link between Machen and McGiehan. The postal official reportedly received a sizable "royalty" payment for the $163,000 worth of package-type boxes purchased when he was the general superintendent of the free delivery service.

It appeared to investigators as though the 1901 contract to McGiehan was manipulated behind the scenes by Machen, who hid his involvement behind a committee to make the actual award. The committee was composed of Thomas B. Marche, chief clerk in the Free Delivery Service, A.B. Hurt, also from that office, and Bernard Goode, chief clerk of the Dead Letter Office. Although the integrity of the three-member committee was never questioned, their actions were suspect because two of them worked for Machen, who reportedly influenced their decision.

In an unrelated case, favoritism and insider information was also suspected by 42 manufacturers of rural mailboxes. They always were outmaneuvered by four other firms that always seemed to secure information about the creation of new routes well in advance of the rest. This enabled the favored foursome to sell their mailboxes to families along the proposed routes before the other companies were even aware that new routes were envisioned. According to allegations published in the May 1903 issue of *The Postmasters' Advocate*, "It is claimed that these favored firms not only get this information concerning the establishment of routes, but that they actually have an agent traveling with the special agent (assigned by the Post Office Department) who lays out the route, and these box agents call on the prospective patrons of the route and tell them that their box is 'the only approved one' and in many cases the unsuspecting farmer buys the box and signs an order therefore, paying an enormous price. These box agents sell a 50 cent box for $2.50, and the farmer pays the tax in order that the 'inner ring' may all get their rake off." Claiming collusion, one company circulated an open letter insisting that "There is no question but what a bribe has been offered and received in this case, and the presumption is that the Groff fastener fraud would pale into insignificance by comparison." In this case, no direct link to Machen was found.

Machen and his co-defendants went on trial during the early winter of 1904 in Washington, D.C. Assistant U.S. Attorney Morgan H. Beach and special counsel Holmes Conrad conducted the prosecution. Defense attorneys included Charles A. Douglass, C.H. Syme and John F. Kumler.

Machen was a good witness. He was called "Unabashed on the stand." He never was at a loss for an answer, although many were terse responses, and he never grew fatigued during cross-examination. At one point, rather than responding to a question, he told the prosecuting attorney, "I'm not a lawyer," to which Holmes Conrad replied, "No, but you've got sense enough to stock a whole bar," a barb aimed at drawing attention to the number of defense attorneys present.

Machen's conduct did not escape the media. One publication reported, "Machen did not make a very good impression on the spectators during the long trial. His flippant treatment of a matter, which proved to be very serious to him, had the opposite effect from that which he evidently intended."

Machen relished teasing prosecutor Holmes Conrad. He initially referred to him as "colonel" when answering his questions. Conrad let this slide for a long time, but finally corrected Machen, advising him that he had been a major. Machen already was well aware of the prosecutor's former military rank. When asked nicely by Conrad to use his correct rank if he wished to continue to refer to any rank at all, Machen replied "Sure" and indicated through elaborate hand gestures that it was all the same to him. From there on out, Machen did his best to overemphasize the title "major" whenever addressing Conrad.

Despite the fact that every detail of the trial was hotly contested by both sides, in the end the prosecution prevailed.

After about nine hours of deliberations the jury rendered its verdict on February 26, 1904. The judgment was "guilty as indicted" for Machen and all but one of the others. Machen was stunned. He called the verdict a "Thunderbolt" and he physically appeared as though he was struck by one. Those in the chamber said Machen turned ghostly pale, appearing "gray and twisted."

Sentencing was that same afternoon. One-by-one the defendants heard the judge's ruling, which was the same for all those rendered guilty. Machen was among the first, an action that was interpreted as recognition of Machen's predominant role in the affair. Whether to prolong his agony, or simply because the presiding judge had momentarily forgotten, the judge hesitated in pronouncing Machen's sentence, asking the U.S. Marshall present in the courtroom instead in a clearly audible tone, "What's the name of that penitentiary?" Machen winced even more than before as he waited for the answer. "Moundsville," whispered the Marshall. "Oh, yes," proclaimed the judge, continuing: "I sentence the defendant, Machen, to two years in the penitentiary at Moundsville (West Virginia), and to pay a fine of $10,000. The imprisonment is to begin with the entrance to the penitentiary." Upon hearing this, Machen looked as if he was near about suffering a stroke. His face instantly turned beet red and then grew deathly pale.

The *Washington Post* viewed the verdict as a "wholesome" outcome. "The conviction of Machen and his accomplices in the conspiracy to defraud the government is the most important incident thus far recorded in the accomplishment of the long and difficult task of unearthing the various crimes in the postal service and bringing their perpetrators to justice. It is a wholesome verdict that convicts these conspirators and a just sentence which will consign them to the penitentiary."

But this was only round one for Machen. He hoped for a reprieve, but that hope was unrealistic. Although Machen quickly moved to appeal his first conviction, which he hoped to overturn, he was also still facing 13 other indictments; charges that were pending for conspiracy in connection with the case involving the painting contracts for package and letterboxes, as well as for bribery associated with the purchase of letter boxes, rural carriers' satchels and straps and rural carrier badges. And in the end he lost all the way around. The U.S. Supreme Court denied Machen's application for a writ of certiorari in the case against him on charges of conspiring to defraud the government. This let stand the decision of the U.S. Court of Appeals for the District of Columbia, finding him guilty as charged.

As Machen was about to return to court on the second bill of indictments in mid-1905, a trial that was expected to be another long and drawn out battle, he surprised everyone by pleading guilty. He did this, he said, to save his family and friends from anymore unpleasantness. "Embarrassed as I am by my present situation and surrounded with all disadvantages which are its consequence, I am from that fact alone in almost a defenseless position. I shall therefore willingly submit to any penalty which the court may deem proper to impose upon me ...," he stated. The court believed that two more years was sufficient.

By the time Machen's prison sentence was served the number of rural routes had grown to about 40,000; and, while the pattern of growth would continue in years to come, nothing like the swindles that Machen tried to carry out would ever again adversely affect the further development of Rural Free Delivery.

EVOLUTIONS

HARDLY ENOUGH

For their efforts, RFD carriers were not well paid. When Leander Sylvester Denius began carrying mail in April 1898 his pay was $300 a year. This, the New Castle, Indiana, carrier figured was "compensation which merely paid for horse feed and axle grease." The salary gradually increased, inching up to about $600 in 1903, but that still wasn't much. By July 1904, the pay was up to $720 annually. Other increases came in 1907, $900; 1911, $1,000; and 1912, $1,100. On July 1, 1914, the pay scale rose to $1,200 for a 24-mile route.

Despite such increases, the wages never seemed to be enough; and the low pay dampened interest in buying motor vehicles. This was the reason why few rural routes were motorized before World War I.

"There's little enough left from my $50 a month salary after operating expenses are paid," said one young carrier in 1903. That comment took into account his bills for having a horse-drawn rural route. He had to pay the bank for the loan to buy his mail wagon and maintain his two horses. Harnesses and blankets, for example, cost $20. Then there was the routine blacksmith's bills of $3 a month, plus feed bills that amounted to $17, and veterinary services that cost $2 a month. The rent on the carrier's home was another $8 a month, leaving next to nothing for groceries and living expenses.

Every carrier held out hopes that conditions would improve. The general sentiment was summed up by Albert Wilson, a carrier from Lovilla, Iowa, when he observed, "Feed has been high for the last two years and this is working a hardship on us carriers who have our feed to buy, but we are in hopes even yet of feed getting cheaper or our salary being raised, or both, but not till some change takes place will the carriers get rich very fast."

Frank Boylen had it better than many ... he wasn't married. "I would get married," said the Indiana carrier, "if I could get enough ahead to get the license and pay the preacher." In all truthfulness this probably was more a case of cold feet than a stinging indictment of the pay scale for carriers. In Iowa horse feed was fairly cheap. Hay was $10 a ton, corn was 45 cents a bushel, and wheat bran was $1.40 per 100 pounds.

In some isolated areas of the country the pay went a little farther than others. Where horses were relatively cheap and forage was abundant, the salary was regarded as barely adequate. In most other areas, the carriers had a hard time making ends meet. "Feed is very high in this part of the country," confessed Texas carrier Curtis E. McMillan in the early 1900s. Prairie hay in Texas was $14 a ton, corn was 75 cents a bushel, and wheat bran was $1.50 for 100 pounds. At the same time in parts of Oregon the price tag for an equines' menu was a bit higher: clover hay was $18 a ton, corn was 95 cents a bushel, and wheat bran was $6.60 per 100 pounds. In sections of Louisiana hay was $25 a ton, corn was $1 a bushel, and bran was $1.60 per 100 pounds. This prompted Lillie, Louisiana, carrier Charlie Rockett to complain "The salary is too small as feed is so high." After a moment of thought, he qualified his response by noting that "everything is high." Maine was also an extremely costly place to be a carrier. Hay there was $18 a ton, corn was $1.60 a bushel and bran was $1.55 per one hundred-pound bag.

Even living on a farm didn't always help. A carrier from another part of the country lamented that "I live on a farm and keep five horses, raise my feed and still I am behind."

Road conditions had a direct correlation between a carrier's ability to balance his budget or not. The worse the roads were ... the more horses a carrier

This 1915 advertisement by the Kearns Motor Truck Co. touted its truck and runabout as a dependable way to deliver mail.

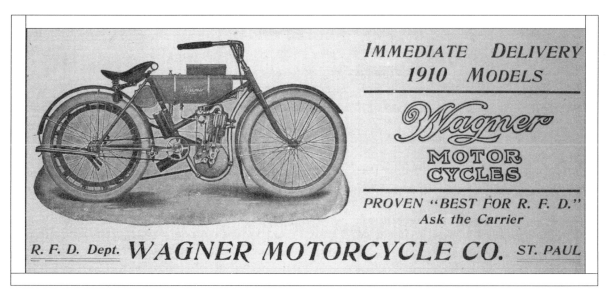

Wagner produced a good motorcycle, but you could not tell from the somewhat modest tone of this advertisement.

needed ... the more it cost to care and feed for the beasts ... the less the carrier had left at the end of the month.

"I keep three horses, and drive two. The roads are too rough for one horse," observed carrier Stacey Taft. If he tried getting by with using a single horse, it would drop dead before the normal day was out. Most of Taft's 25-mile wagon route was rough going. "I (don't) have more than one-half mile of worked road on the route," he told his colleagues in the early 1900s. He would simply follow the tracks he made the day before in the mud flows as best he could, except for a brief half-mile section that he had to ford. "There you guess at it and if it gets too deep, (you) back out and stay until the water goes down."

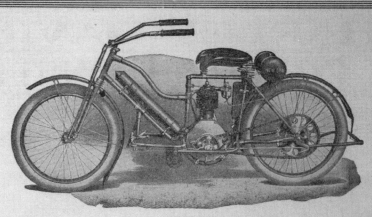
The New Era Auto-cycle Company used this advertisement in 1911 to attract the attention of rural letter carriers.

An Iowa carrier couldn't quite figure out how the mileage was calculated. "My route is 26-1/2 miles, if it were level, but it is up and down hills. I have 53 ups and 52 downs, two gumbo river bottoms and 17 hills of the roll up, stick tight, never slip clay wax (type)."

"I have spent nearly everything to keep my route," observed North Carolina carrier Major Predgen. That included $601 for horses and $640 for feed and vet bills, leaving him little for family food, cloths, rent and firewood. Part of Predgen's problem was that he went through horses fairly fast. By 1908, he had worn out 22 different horses and mules on his 27-mile route during a three-year period. Predgen blamed it all on the roads he was forced to cover. He said that they were all mud, with an ample supply of tree stumps and pot holes thrown in for good measure.

During his five year tenure, Walter Taylor wore out 14 horses. "I have five big hills of red clay about knee deep and I cross one creek four times," said

the West Virginia carrier in describing why he went through so many horses.

A contemporary of Taylor's, John Janson, a carrier from Spokane, Washington, believed the same way. "The roads have been awful lately and my ponies have been played out everyday," he said.

Of course, not all horses pulled the same weight. Horses were typically hitched together in teams of twos or switched half way through the day to keep them from keeling over from exhaustion. But some horses were near worthless when it came to hard work. "I have five horses," confessed one Oklahoma carrier in 1908. "Three are good ones and two are plugs." Dealing with the two dragged-out horses was enough of a burden for the carrier to admit that "You will never know of me buying a plug again for any purpose. They can eat as much as a good horse, and can do but little hard driving."

New York carrier Bert Steele felt the same way. He typically was a good judge of horse flesh, but at least once he got burned on a horse trade. He

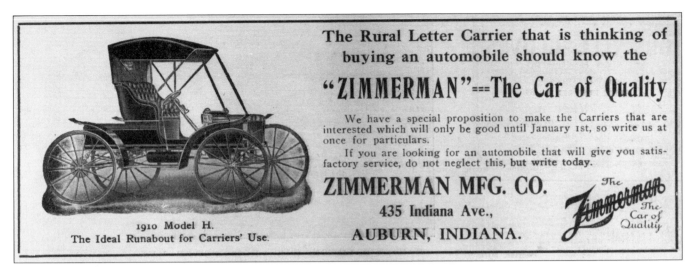

Zimmerman Manufacturing Company wanted rural carriers to think of its car as "The Car of Quality."

briefly used one horse on his Pierrepont Manor route, but it was a real nag. "I remember getting a horse from a man that was in the habit of visiting the local hotel quite frequently. I had to blindfold (the horse) to get him past that place for more than two weeks." Steele got rid of the horse in short order.

Oklahoma carrier John Kennedy typically got everything out of his horses that he could. He got rid of his horses only as a last resort. The early 1900s carrier sold one of the oldest horses used on his route for a mere 67 cents. The price may seem low, but one of Kennedy's acquaintances explained away the petty sum by observing that John "got most of the good (use) out (of the horse) before he sold (it!)"

Carriers tried to cut corners wherever possible. "I do my own horseshoeing, in fact, I have to in order to make anything," said a carrier in the early 1900s. This practice wore heavily on his conscience, causing him to confess to his fellow carriers that "I really hate to 'scab' on the town's blacksmith, but it can't be helped."

There were other expenses. Carriers were required to give a bond equivalent to $500, as were their substitutes. In no instance was mail to be handled by an unbonded carrier.

There were other conditions of employment that, while they didn't have a monetary price tag, caused carriers to live in a fish bowl. Carriers had to be of good character and temperance. They were to be neat and tidy and free of any criminal record.

There were no restrictions on gender, and a few women became rural carriers, some as substitutes

for their husbands, others on their own accord. By 1904, 105 carriers were women. Oddly enough in an age where men were seen as the principal wage earners, women carriers received the same pay as men.

The salary of the early carriers was dependent upon the length of their route. The typical wagon route was 24 miles. Carriers with routes under 24 miles got less pay, depending on the length of their route.

Although the issue of higher pay was already an ongoing bit of old business by 1908, Wisconsin carrier F.E. Edwards griped that his route was slightly more than 26 miles, but he wasn't properly compensated for the added distance. "I hope Congress will do something this session and allow us the extra (pay for the added miles) we have to travel over 24 miles, if nothing more," he said. Congress would ultimately get around to this issue—eight years later!

In the intervening years one thing became clear; on good days some carriers could finish fairly fast. This irked postal officials who in 1916 testified before Congress that carriers who used automobiles or motorcycles in particular could complete their rounds in under two hours. Fourth Assistant Postmaster General James I. Blakslee told Congress that motorized carriers "enjoy a joy ride every day and get $1,200 a year for it." This prompted him to ask, "Do you call it a fair day's work when covered in two hours?" Blakslee didn't think so. He thought a full day's work was due. "I think if the carrier has done eight hours of labor from the time he enters upon his daily duty of distributing his mail until the

SAXON ROADSTER $395

Cheaper for you than a horse and buggy

Use a Saxon for your R. F. D. work—Price $395.

There was a time when the horse and buggy was the only practical conveyance for R. F. D. men. Today the horse and buggy is still good—but the Saxon is cheaper—more economical—more comfortable—more efficient in every respect than any other conveyance, and R. F. D. men all over the country are turning their eyes toward this car—discarding their old equipment—buying Saxons.

Efficiency is as important to the R. F. D. man as it is to the salesman. To be thoroughly efficient you should be able to make your daily trips regardless of weather or road conditions. You should not vary several hours each day in the delivery of mail—Saxon will enable you to maintain a schedule.

With the horse and buggy it is impossible to make time covering your route, even when conditions are ideal. With the Saxon roadster you can make your daily trip under any condition. You can make it more quickly and in more comfort than with any other conveyance. You get home earlier. You might take a longer route and make more money.

Saxon sturdiness and dependability have been proved through actual demonstration. Read what Saxon cars have done.

100 Saxon dealers from 100 towns throughout the United States drove Saxon roadsters in 200-mile non-stop runs. Each car was driven 200 miles without the motor being stopped. The world's economy record of 34.5 miles per gallon of gasoline was established.

Saxon roadster was the first car to cross the continent over the Lincoln Highway. It crossed thirteen States in thirty days, covering 3,389 miles. Thirty miles per gallon of gasoline was averaged.

The Saxon roadster was driven across the snow capped Rocky Mountains in the dead of winter. It traveled a distance of 1,385 miles over mountain roads that are extremely dangerous in summer and practically impassable in winter.

Saxon roadsters made a thirty-day run of 4,500 miles between New York and Albany; a thirty-day run of 6,000 miles between Boston and Springfield; a thirty-day run of 4,500 miles over country roads near Detroit.

Saxon roadster was driven from Tiffin, Ohio, to Los Angeles, California. The entire expense, including gasoline, oil, incidentals, was only $38.60.

These are only a few records showing the Saxon's durability.

In no other car on the market at anywhere near the Saxon price can you get all these modern features: 3-speed transmission—Timken axles—high speed type motor—handsome roomy body—honey-comb radiator—dry plate clutch — Atwater-Kent ignition — cantilever springs of vanadium steel—adjustable pedals.

Find out about this car. Ask your Saxon dealer to take you around your route in a Saxon roadster. If you don't know the name of the nearest dealer—write us. Ask, too, for a copy of "Saxon Days." Address Dept. 29.

Saxon Delivery Car $395

If you prefer a light delivery car for your R. F. D. work—we recommend the Saxon delivery car. Its carrying capacity is 400 pounds, besides driver's weight. Its body height is 49¼ inches—its length 37 inches (back of driver's seat). It has storm curtains at the sides for use in bad weather. It has the same sturdy mechanical features of the Saxon roadster—high speed motor—3-speed transmission—Timken axles—cantilever springs—and so on. Ask your dealer about this car.

SAXON MOTOR CAR CORPORATION, Detroit, Mich.

(230)

A 1915 advertisement for the Saxon roadster.

time he is relieved from duty, he has performed a fair day's work."

There was a line in the sand, and Blakslee had crossed it! Blakslee was immediately accused of unfairly bashing the carriers. The heat got so intense that he was forced to momentarily recant somewhat. "Rural letter carriers are not goldbricking the public," he hesitantly acknowledged. But he really hadn't changed his mind. In short order he was back on the attack. "I shall continue to demand for the rural carriers a fair day's pay for a fair day's work."

Blakslee played on the public sentiment, while at the same time taking his attack directly to the carriers. "You can cover your (motorized) routes in two, three, or four hours and collect $1,200 a year, but you cannot make your friends and neighbors ... believe that you earned it," he told a group of rural carriers in Memphis, Tennessee, on February 22, 1916.

The view of finishing in only a couple of hours was all well and good in the summer months, but it was unrealistic during January through March for most of the country. Blakslee fudged the issue of whether the work could be done within eight hours during the winter months. His position was that the only way to resolve this was to lengthen routes from 25 to 50 miles. This would be a great deal of savings, considering there were over 42,000 rural carriers nationwide and about one-tenth were assigned to motorized routes.

The bottom line was that the length of the route was more important than the time on the clock, especially since Blakslee wanted to convert as many slower horse-drawn routes to motorized routes as possible, while upping the distance that was to be covered.

Blakslee's logic reflected his boss' thinking. Postmaster General Albert Burleson was a fanatic when it came to time/management efficiencies, standardization and party politics. Burleson replaced 5,765 postmasters within the first 176 days of the Wilson administration. Of these postings, 2,203 were "Presidential Postmasters," office-holders who received in excess of $1,000 annually and whose political appointments had to be confirmed by the Senate. With a loyal crew in place, Burleson began to squeeze greater efficiency out of the postal system. Morale meant nothing and neither did tenure. He wanted to force postal employees to work longer and harder—at no additional cost—and he particularly wanted older workers to go. It was charged that he especially wanted to get rid of all old-time Republicans, which was somewhat true, as well as all Union Army veterans, which was never really proven, although the unsympathetic press had a field day with that particular allegation. The gist of the outrage was captured by the Baldwin City (Kansas) *Ledger*, which observed that the Burleson administration "recently attracted nationwide attention by the wholesale manner in which (it) decapitated clerks and carriers in the Washington (D.C.) post office who were found guilty of wearing

Thiem's claimed to have the cheapest and best motorcycles available for government.

the old bronze button and in connection therewith having given too many years of faithful service to Uncle Sam." According to the paper, "Protests from Grand Army of the Republic posts were of no avail, for their voting strength is not as great as it used to be and the South is strictly in the saddle."

In one respect, what Burleson was accused of made good financial sense. Dismissals or demoting older Republican workers, paid $1,200, in exchange for good young Democrats, at $800 apiece, represented quite a savings. It was said that this action saved as much as $90,000 in the cost of running the Washington post office. This prompted the *St. Louis Globe-Democrat* to charge that some of his "petty economies have been rendered possible by demoting veteran clerks, who have spent their lives in the service."

Burleson's actions drove rank-and-file postal workers crazy. He went so far as to have supervisors walk around postal facilities and trail rural carriers with stopwatches or other time measuring devices to determine how well postal people were working. This sort of thing was overtly or covertly opposed by workers, and it was scorned by members of Congress, including one representative who introduced a bill to put a stop to such practices.

He also made a mockery of the eight-hour law passed in the Taft administration. For his attempts to spread the work of an eight hour day out over as much as 12 hours, Burleson was accused in the press of being "tyrannical" and of "Russianizing the (postal) service." He also was labeled as "a visionary theorist without proper knowledge of the needs of the service or conditions under which service is to be rendered." The Sisseton, South Dakota, *Weekly Standard* was blunt in its assessment of Burleson's ideas, stating that he had a "lack of horse sense in the management of his department."

Another common sentiment during the Burleson era was that rural carriers were treated as second-class workers. City carriers, for example, not only received larger salaries than their rural counterparts, they also did not have to furnish their own vehicles. Postal clerks, on the other hand, typically worked inside somewhat comfortable facilities, away from the icy elements. And when conditions inside post offices were poor, the clerks usually had enough clout to make things better. When postal clerks in the nation's capital complained of poor working conditions, the Congress responded by building a new post office. These facts failed to escape rural carriers. They wanted a degree of equity. "Let us hope," wrote one rural American in the years before World War I, "that the same considerations which prompted Congress to refuse to add to

the burdens of Washington government clerks will be exercised on behalf of another class of government employees, namely, rural carriers, who do not work in comfortable offices, and are not afforded convenient shelter from the vicissitudes and inclemencies (sic) of the season, but must render their service out in the open, regardless of weather or road conditions."

The postmaster general seemed to have a virtual disregard for the old adage that when you are in a hole, the first thing you do is stop digging. Instead, his self-made morass seemed to only get deeper and deeper. Another of his schemes, to double the length of rural routes and to require carriers to use automobiles, was quick to attract lightning. Newspapers around the country advised their readers that, while that sort of service might work in the outskirts of the nation's capital (where it really didn't either), it wasn't really practical in places where roads were covered with drifting snow for as much as four months of the year.

Some carriers and their patrons argued that it wasn't so much a matter of how long one served as much as where. Burleson's idea of efficiency failed to take into account one simple truth: Each rural route was different in terms of terrain and soil types; therefore, each had to have its own timetable, dependent principally upon the weather for dry and wet times, and the road conditions. Every carrier realized this. They also knew that different vehicles worked on different routes. Iowa carrier G.R. Walrath, a motorcycle user, believed that he was using the only practical means of moving the mail. A wagon was out of the question, he thought, and an automobile was questionable over what he called "28-1/2 miles of Iowa's stickiest and blackest roads, with a few yellow clay hills to break the monotony." Said Walrath, "I have never used an auto, as owing to the condition of the soil and poorly-graded roads an auto could not be used to exceed seven months during the year, at most. There is no sand in the soil here, and no gravel roads. The roads are all built of dirt, clay or muck, and a 30 minute rain will change a road from a pavement to a hog wallow." Other carriers swore by automobiles, buggies or wagons, depending upon the circumstances surrounding their particular routes.

Farmers understood the difference between service in wet and dry seasons, even if postal officials such as Blakslee didn't want to let on that they knew it too. Farmers took exception to the notion of a uniform eight hour day. One planter, writing to the Arlington, Texas, *Farmers' Fireside Bulletin*, asserted that, as a whole, farmers "would prefer to

Resourceful rural carriers used a variety of vehicles, depending on climate and terrain, but this three-wheeler was never popular, despite the "free" come-on.

have (delivery times) shortened where it is necessary to be able to get the mail in the forenoon in dry weather," and not lengthened. To make this possible, carriers almost had to use motorcycles or automobiles during the summer months, while the length of the routes remained at the 24-mile limit. Such farmers were reasonable. "Of course, we could not expect them to make it that early in wet weather, but we (would) soon learn about what time to expect him when it is muddy and he has to use a horse."

Blakslee countered by saying that the postal system was being inundated with telegrams urging that the 50-mile motorized routes be established as soon as possible. Farm families and legislatures saw through this ploy in a minute. The telegrams were largely from postmasters interested in earning points for backing Blakslee's pet project. Rural residents hoped that Congress would put a stop to such thinking.

At one point Blakslee wanted tangible proof that he could exploit with the press, so he assigned an agent to hitch a ride with a motorized carrier. Unfortunately, this little scheme backfired too, because the inspector arrived on the wrong day. Instead of completing the route within eight hours, mail volumes were heavy and road conditions were poorer than anticipated for a dry month, causing the ride to last nearly 12 hours. The ride-along started at 8:30 a.m. and went on until 8 p.m., proving that in this case automobiles provided no savings over a 50-mile route. This prompted the *Philadelphia North American* to report, "Fourth Assistant Postmaster General Blakslee may be compelled to give up his pet scheme of rural auto routes in some sections as a matter of political expediency."

Congress was quickly drawn into the issue. One congressman believed that the weight of the mail and the distance traveled should control the carriers' pay. "I think that any other basis in the world

International Harvester was one of the first manufacturers to design a special automotive body for a rural mail vehicle. This advertisement appeared in 1912.

would be unfair." But, he cautioned, "I do think the $1,200, the maximum for a 24-mile route, taking into consideration the sparsely settled sections of the country, is pretty good pay for rural carriers (on a horse-drawn route)." Other legislators believed that the compensation should be nearly double that.

Unfortunately for him, one of Blakslee's biggest problems was that he didn't know when to quit. He repeatedly clashed with key members of Congress over various large and small issues. Typical of his bravado was his questioning of several senators over their support of certain sections of the Post Office appropriations bill, aspects that he didn't particularly like. He accused the senators of selling out to the railroads. This was like throwing a match on gasoline. The senators blew up at Blakslee. One said "Mr. Blakslee's letters were extremely offensive to me personally, and as a United States Senator, I look upon the words 'surrender to the railroads' as an insult, nothing more and nothing less .... This sort of thing is bad enough from a private citizen

and would be a serious matter, but it is far more censurable when it comes from a Department executive who should help rather than hinder us. The Post Office Committee cannot ignore or even condone such an attack." Postmaster General Burleson shielded Blakslee as best he could, but from then on many of the members of the Senate Post Office Committee were out for Blakslee's scalp. The Committee repeatedly called for his resignation, but Blakslee survived until 1921 when Warren G. Harding's administration brought in a whole new crew of senior postal officials.

Burleson had other, more personal problems to contend with. Assertions of irregularities in some of his business dealings before being appointed as postmaster general surfaced at about the same time. What struck postal workers as odd was how they were being paid peanuts while their "fat cat" postmaster general had apparently made out handily by exploiting "the system." Members of the Senate launched an investigation in 1916 against Burleson's alleged use of convicts to farm his property in

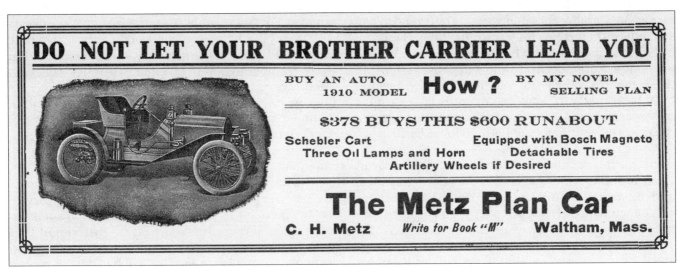

Rural carriers were offered "great deals" on a variety of new vehicles. This was done in the hopes that it would promote sales among rural mail patrons.

Texas a few years earlier. The Burleson and Johns Farm, a splendid tract of 5,000 acres bordering on Hill and Bosque counties, was cultivated by approximately 80 state convicts; prisoners who were allegedly beaten, tortured, and killed for the slightest infraction. Burleson and the state shared in the proceeds from the convict-labor cotton farm. Sixty percent went to Texas and 40 percent to Burleson and Johns, a relative of Burleson's. The senator who raised the issue said, "Out of such labor, out of such profits from a State convict, out of such a tainted source, Postmaster General Burleson has become the wealthiest member of the Democratic cabinet today." The senator said that he wasn't sure if the information was known at the time of Burleson's appointment to head up the postal system, but that "It will not be unknown from now afterwards." Perhaps the worst attack to come out of this was the charge concerning Burleson's involvement in the treatment of Thomas Durham. The one-time state foreman at the farm, Durham was indicted for the death of one of the convicts. Tried in 1911, Durham was subsequently acquitted because the state could produce nothing against him but the testimony of African American inmates. Two years after Durham's acquittal, Burleson is said to have seen to it that he was appointed postmaster of Longview, Texas. According to the senator who brought the charges, this outraged the Congressman from that district, as well as a large number of the leading families of the community. But Burleson had his way. Durham remained as postmaster until his death a year later. Burleson did not appreciate such asser-

The Model K Schacht was characterized as "The Carrier's Friend--Always Ready and Dependable."

tions and he did not take them lying down. He quickly called for such statements to be retracted, labeling all the charges "vilely false." Burleson's version was that he was only a part owner of the plantation which the state leased and operated, and that the foreman referred to was the plantation superintendent employed by the state, and who was acquitted of a charge that was believed to have been made for political purposes. About the only other difference between the two sides was the way in which Durham was appointed as postmaster. Burleson contended that it was made with the acquiescence of the congressman from his district.

With respect to the issue of postal pay, cooler heads on Capitol Hill prevailed. "The standard of schedules should not only have included January, but should have included July and May ... and October and November, so that a fair average of all these months under the varying conditions would have been reached," said one member of the House of Representatives. This was fast becoming typical of the majority sentiments of both political parties.

Growing tired of all the fuss, Georgia Senator Thomas Hardwick introduced an amendment early in 1916 that limited horse-drawn routes to 24 miles, and motorized routes to 50 miles. This measure was enacted on July 28, 1916, and was ordered into effect by the postmaster general on August 15, 1916. This measure eliminated the advantages enjoyed by motorized carriers over their colleagues who relied on horseflesh, benefits that enabled them to finish work faster. The action also had some cost consequences in that it authorized the postmaster general to increase the length of horse-drawn routes by up to 50 percent, provided carriers were compensated at a rate of $24 annually for each additional mile over the 24-mile standard.

In most summer months the nation's rural carriers could indeed gain some time, hours that could be devoted to other outside employment or work around the house. But in the winter, when routes might not be finished until well after dark, if at all, the time gains were pretty much brought back into balance by uncompensated overtime requirements.

Carrier salaries continued to increase—along with rising costs—going to $1,500 by July 1919, with a $300 increase the following year. And, much to the relief of postal employees, with the election of Warren G. Harding, Will Hays replaced Albert Burleson as postmaster general. Hays tried to rebuild morale and to humanize the postal service. One of his initiatives, conducted in conjunction with the U.S. Public Health Service, was to authorize rural carriers and parcel post truck drivers to weigh infants using the scales on their vehicles. This practice allowed mothers to keep track of their childrens' growth. This modest effort was extremely well received. Unfortunately, Hays stayed only one year.

Poorly paid carriers were creative about how they supplemented their income. Although the Post Office Department did not sanction or condone such moonlighting, some rural carriers distributed advertising cards that informed patrons that sideline errands could be done in exchange for goods, such as eggs, or money. Actually there were a lot of takers. Typical of this shop-at-home service, one carrier received a good-sized grocery list, asking him to purchase sugar, coffee, prunes, cookies and steaks. For his trouble the carrier got 10 cents.

Others took in outside work from those they served. A bit out of the ordinary, one such card from New Hampshire even boasted "Laundry collected Monday, returned Saturday."

Low pay wasn't the only problem carriers had to contend with. RFD was not incorporated under the Civil Service system until shortly after the turn of the century. Prior to that, politics and nepotism influenced many appointments.

Early on, customer perceptions were problematic. Not everyone fully understood what RFD service really included. This confusion resulted in some really unusual requests. Some fleetingly thought that this new carrier service represented some grand scheme to employ roving odd jobs, people whose principal task was to deliver the mail, but who could accommodate other incidentals. This misconception caused one farm wife to ask her new carrier to wring out her laundry, wash what was soaking in the washtub on the porch, and hang it on the washline. Another carrier received this note, which was more typical of the kind of chores you would ask a field hand to do: "Please feed our chickens and water the cows and the mule in the stable and if the bees have swarmed put them in a new hive. We have gone visiting."

As one might expect, there has always been a special relationship between the carriers and the families along their route. Often, if a carrier was a young, eligible fellow, the daughters of farmers would greet him at the mailbox with freshly baked goods. This was their way of showing off their cooking skills. Besides, you have to remember that the RFD carrier was obviously a "good catch" because he owned his own vehicle—which was ideal whenever there were community dances or church socials—and he had a steady income.

Young carriers had to be careful about how they handled such attentions. Nothing could bring a postal inspector faster than a report that the carrier was dallying with a young lady along his route.

When it came to poor pay, rural carriers weren't alone. All postal employees had to be patient when it came to pay increases. Uncle Sam was stingy, but few realized how tightfisted until 1920 when Congress heard one horror story after another during joint committee testimony. Forty-five percent of the city letter carriers in Boston were estimated to have been in hock to loan sharks; about 60 percent of the railway mail clerks in New York were in debt; approximately 50 percent of the workers in the New Haven post office had to work second jobs to make ends meet; and over one-half of the clerks in Hartford, Connecticut, couldn't get by on their postal pay. Moonlighting among postal workers was commonplace. Things were so bad that in 1920 one old-time worker said, "No man in the postal service today would willingly consent to his son entering it."

Nearly 50 years later, little had changed. Starting salaries for postal workers in 1969 was $6,176. This was well below the $11,236 that the federal government estimated was needed to "moderately" maintain a family of four in New York City. A surprising number of postal workers were receiving public assistance or were working two or more jobs, in addition to their full-time salaries. Crueler still, postal workers had to face the reality that they were paid about $4,000 less than some sanitation department employees.

The poor pay made it difficult for rural carriers to afford their own automobile or truck. By 1916, there were only 438 auto routes nationwide, with another 671 authorized. In addition, over 8,000 other routes involved the use of motorcycles.

Motorcycle manufacturers had been enticing rural carriers since the early 1900s with claims of speed, reliability and low operating costs. The maker of the Excelsior motorcycle boasted that it made "The greatest motorcycle ever built," while Harley-Davidson claimed that the expense of operating its motorcycles was "Less than one-third that of team or auto."

While motorcycles briefly held the greater share of the market, that would change by the end of World War I.

Cars and trucks were more expensive; and somehow the cost seemed worth it, especially to the public and the press. One newspaper went so far as to state that "whenever the motor car has been used, its superiority has been fully demonstrated. That it is cheaper than the horse and vehicle hitherto used seems to be well established."

No time was wasted ... no opportunities were missed. As soon as motorized mail routes were authorized automakers began wooing rural carriers for their business.

Auto manufacturers began pressing rural letter carriers for sales in earnest in the early 1900s. Their advertisements began as small displays in such publications as *R.F.D. News*. By 1908, the "come-ons" included boasts by Chicago Motor Buggy that its "Chicago" model was "An ideal vehicle for Rural Carriers" or W.H. McIntyre that its 14-hp model "Runs under all conditions."

The Mier Carriage and Buggy Co. called its 1908 Model A runabout "A practical machine for rural mail service." This was a somewhat more truthful pitch than most, because few such vehicles were really practical on poorly maintained backwoods roads or when it rained. And the Mier Model A was no exception. Weighing in at about 1,000 pounds, and powered as it was by a two-cylinder engine, it was easy prey for any messy gumbo-like path.

J.V. Lindsley and Co. also played it safe by claiming that its 10-hp "Lindsley Car" would run through any sand, mud or snow and will climb any hill "within reason."

Despite the array of claims—and the advertising copy often sounded overly impressive—in reality there didn't seem to be a great deal of difference between most models in the early 1900s. Most early automobile manufacturers offered vehicles with about the same basic characteristics: buggy styling and a two-cylinder engine that generated about 10 to 14 hp.

As the automotive industry came of age in the 1910s and 1920s more and more cars and light trucks were being used for rural service. By the mid-1920s, horse-drawn RFD vehicles had fast become a thing of the past.

EVOLUTIONS

ANYTHING FOR A SALE

Beginning in 1906, the Post Office Department started its own brand of automotive affirmative action, setting aside a growing proportion of rural mail routes as "auto routes." These were either new routes or replacements for horse-drawn service.

In either case, the growing number of routes was sweet nectar to carmakers who swarmed over the potential ranks of the soon-to-be-motorized carriers with all sorts of sales pitches.

Most of the earliest automobiles used by rural letter carriers offered the same basic features: a simple two-cylinder engine that was capable of producing 10 to 15 hp, got 30 mpg, and had solid "puncture proof" rubber tires as well as buggy-like styling.

Another similarity was that said vehicles also were largely produced by companies that disappeared within a few years, firms such as A.B.C. Motor Vehicle Co. or J.V. Lindsley. The pitch line for A.B.C. was "a simple name, (a) simple machine," while Lindsley's claim was "No Bother—No Fussing—No Cussing." Given its lack of longevity, perhaps Lindsley should have added a fourth—"No

Servicing"—because it was out of business within one year.

One of the greatest selling points about these early vehicles was their ground clearance and wagon-style wheels. For rural letter carriers, especially those who were raised on a farm or were switching from horse-drawn to motorized vehicles, a wagon-style wheel was highly reassuring. In fact, the bigger the wheels the better. For snowy or muddy routes, a road clearance of 18 inches was considered a major selling point.

Truth in advertising was not a strong point among many of these firms. Many overstated the ability of their vehicles. The Schacht Manufacturing Co. of Cincinnati, Ohio, for example, claimed that its 1908 Model K "will go anywhere wheels will travel." Of course this ad made no distinction between good and bad road conditions. At the same time, the King Motor Vehicle Co. of Auburn, Indiana, went even further, stating that its RFD motor wagon was "the most practical motor wagon in the world for mail carriers." King also boasted that its 12-hp, two-cylinder, air-cooled, double-chain-drive

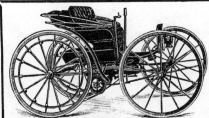

A 1903 advertisement for the Holsman, "especially adapted for R.F.D. use."

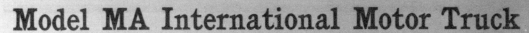

Model MA International Motor Truck
With Air-Cooled Engine—Special for Motor Rural Routes

More than meets every Government requirement. 1,000 pounds capacity, 90 cubic feet space. Stout screen that locks securely. Price only

$655 f. o. b. Akron, Ohio

Your success with the new motor route depends upon a reliable truck that will make its trip every day over country roads regardless of weather conditions.

Specify Model MA International Motor Truck when you take the examination.

It is the right truck at the right price. Other models 1,000, 1,500 and 2,000 pounds capacity, with water-cooled engines. Write for full information.

INTERNATIONAL HARVESTER COMPANY OF AMERICA
(Incorporated)

132 Harvester Building   *Branch Houses in 87 Principal Cities*   Chicago U S A

R.F.D. advertisement for the 1915 Model MA International Motor Truck.

Standard rural mail truck proposed by Postmaster General Albert Burleson in 1915.

Model A was capable of running through deep mud and sand and could climb steep hills with no difficulty.

In the hopes of making sales, each company did its best to outdo the others' claims, but more often than not rural carriers made their selections based on proven reliability and price. Word-of-mouth and testimonials printed in publications such as *R.F.D. News* or the *Postmasters Advocate* were extremely influential, but price was a critical factor in the final

Not all vehicles fall into nice, neat niches. This is especially true when it comes to those used for Rural Free Delivery. Rural carriers used nearly every type of vehicle imaginable. The same is true of the vehicles used by mail contractors. For this reason, only a select number of the more "typical" types have been selected for inclusion in this work.

selection. In 1908, the prices ranged from about $375 for a stripped-down 12-hp Chicago motor buggy to about $680 for a Schacht, but these were little more than motorized buggies.

These vehicles offered no storage capacity to speak of, and not much in the way of amenities for the driver in case of foul weather.

Touring cars soon proved to be one of the principal types of vehicle used by most carriers, but even these had limitations when it came to the safety of the mail. In most cases the mail was simply piled into the back seat.

Standardization never really did occur. About the closest thing to some sort of standardization occurred in 1915. Besides being despised by employees for his heavy-handed management style, Postmaster General Albert Burleson was disliked for his efforts to standardize everything. His standardization campaign included mailboxes, workers' badges, postal locks, mail sacks and postal vehicles.

One part of this was a push to create a standard type of small RFD mail truck. His ideal vehicle was a small, screened truck with a minimum cargo space of 80 feet. The design was approved by Burleson in September 1915, but his action had no teeth. The design was simply passed along to each new motorized rural carrier as a suggestion. No particular make of chassis was specified, nor was there any compulsion to use the suggested body style. The only thing the new carriers received was a drawing of the vehicle. What was clear though, was that the carrier was expected to pay for the new style truck. This kind of outlay was impossible on a rural carrier's meager wages. For this reason the idea was ignored.

Rural carriers continued to use an assortment of motor vehicles, such as the Model MA screen-side truck by International Harvester, which came about as close to Burleson's standards as possible, while still having the high wheels rural letter carriers preferred.

EVOLUTIONS

WHEN TWO WHEELS
WERE NOT ALLOWED

For a carrier making $900 a year, the maximum salary in 1908 for a 25-mile route, acquiring and maintaining his horse and wagon typically consumed as much as $500 annually, leaving $400 for family needs. That worked out to $1.25 a day, which was less than the cheapest unskilled laborer earned. Under the circumstances, some carriers began to seriously consider using motorcycles.

And those that used them praised their cycles. They were cheap, fast, and maneuverable, as was evident from frequent comments published in *R.F.D. News*, the weekly magazine of the National Rural Letter Carriers' Association. According to one carrier, writing in the early 1900s, "I use a Harley-Davidson three-speed and am getting along pretty well with the work ...." Another carrier, Walter C. Turner at Sutherland, Nebraska, boasted, "I have used both horses and autos and have never felt as completely satisfied as I do now (with a motorcycle). My route extends over 34 miles of roads made up of steep, long hills, trail roads, stretches of loose white sand and river bottom mud."

By the late 1900s, more and more rural carriers were using motorcycles, especially those whose routes were over fairly good terrain and whose customers did not receive over 6,500 pieces of mail a month. And there were plenty of different makes and models to choose from, including cycles by firms such as Wagner Motorcycle Co. (St. Paul), Harley-Davidson Motor Co. (Milwaukee), Excelsior Supply Co. (Chicago), Hornecker Motor Manufacturing Co. (Genesea, Illinois), Consolidated Manufacturing Co. (Toledo, Ohio) and Aurora Automatic Machine Co. (Aurora, Illinois).

By a joint resolution of Congress, passed on March 2, 1915, salaries of rural carriers fell into several nice and neat categories according to the length of the routes they served. Carriers that furnished and maintained their own motor vehicles and served on routes of not less than 50 miles were paid the most. Their fixed salary was $1,800 annually. From this amount, there was a drop-off to $1,200, which applied to routes 24-miles or more. After that, other pay categories included: 22 to 24 miles, $1,152; 20 to 22 miles, $1,080; 18 to 20 miles, $960; 16 to 18 miles, $840; 14 to 16 miles,

Most carriers and their patrons viewed motorcycles as proof of progress. Some postal officials didn't agree.

$720; 12 to 14 miles, $672; 10 to 12 miles, $624; 8 to 10 miles, $526; 6 to 8 miles, $528; and 4 to 6 miles, $480.

If the distances of routes and salaries were fixed, the only remaining variable in making money was speed ... and motorcycles were the fastest and most economical way to move the mail.

For these reasons many carriers preferred motorcycles. The two-wheelers enabled carriers to qualify for longer routes, which paid the most money, and then to finish those routes in near record time, which further allowed carriers to get other part-time jobs to supplement their incomes, or do chores around the house if they wished; or, perhaps more importantly as one carrier observed, it "means hot dinners home at noon instead of a cold lunch on the road." They were so popular that of the nation's approximately 43,000 rural carriers in 1915, almost 8,000 rode motorcycles.

Many carriers claimed that they could complete their routes in roughly three hours using motorcycles. This was approximately half the time it took to cover the same distance by wagon or cart. This typically included serving about 100 mailboxes spread out over a 24-mile distance. Heckman Allen of Neusc, North Carolina, was one such carrier. He reported that he could cover his 26-mile route in anywhere from two-and-one-half to three-and-one-half hours.

Carriers also claimed that it cost less than a quarter of the amount to own a motorcycle than to feed a horse ($5 versus $20 a month) and they didn't have to feed the cycle on off days or when it needed repairs, they just let the two-wheeler sit.

Carrier Elbert Angler from Litchfield, Massachusetts, used this Wagner motorcycle in 1910. On a good day he typically could complete his 29-mile route in just over two hours.

The average life expectancy of a horse was five years. The replacement cost was about $125. As far as tires were concerned, they cost about as much as shoeing a horse. These savings amounted to about $15 to $30 a month in extra spendable cash.

Motorcycle makers hammered away at the economy of their products over other forms of motor vehicles. "From the standpoint of the government we believe that automobile routes will be a success because it will reduce expenses to the government," said Harley-Davidson. And, the cycle makers added, "Whether it will result in as good service is a very big question, but there is one thing we feel sure of and that is from the point of income to the carriers, the routes covered by automobiles cannot be a success, because the average cost per mile will be in excess of six cents." According to motorcycle manufacturer's calculations, the average cost per mile of a motorcycle was between one and two cents. The message to carriers was clear. If they intended to have a motorized route and they wanted to maximize their income, they better use a motorcycle. This line of reasoning was repeated over and over again. Perhaps the thrust of this rationale was summed up in 1915 by Win H. Reel, when he observed, "Cars are all right if money is no object, but give me a motorcycle for economy."

The appeal of motorcycles changed somewhat with the introduction of parcel post. Almost overnight mail volumes became so heavy that cycle carriers had to make two or three trips a day. Others chose to overload the cycles as much as possible. This resulted in all sorts of bizarre bagging, bundling, and stacking techniques.

Motorcycles had one great flaw ... there was no natural place to put the mail. This was fine when the mail was light, as in the case of this route where the mail fit nicely in the carrier's pouch.

The Indian "Big Twin" motorcycle was particularly popular among postal workers. The saddlebag arrangement was well-suited for transporting mail.

Despite such drawbacks, there were times when only a motorcycle would do. When flood waters cut off "Spud" Nordstrom's ability to ford a swollen California river in January 1916, he pushed his two-wheeler up onto a railroad bridge and rode bumpety-bump across the ties. No other type of postal vehicle would have worked in crossing the torrents.

But such "save-the-day" stories didn't sway Albert Burleson. He became Postmaster General on March 5, 1913, and he hated motorcycles. He saw them as woefully unsuited for service, despite the fact that they were inexpensive to operate. They also conflicted with his idea of standardization.

But above all else, they conflicted with his scheme for greater postal efficiency. Burleson was a strong-willed Texan who wanted to squeeze every drop of efficiency out of the postal system that he possibly could. Burleson was a firm believer in the value of efficiency and such things as time/motion studies. Such "tools" were then very much the rage with "enlightened" managerial types, such as Burleson. He certainly was a bit more zealous than most of his predecessors on this point. Efficiency

wasn't a bad idea, especially for the nation's largest civilian employer, but Burleson took things a bit too far. He had supervisors go around postal routes and through facilities with stopwatches and other time measuring devices to determine how well postal people were working. This was overtly and covertly opposed by workers, and such practices were scorned by members of Congress, including one representative who introduced a bill to put a stop to such practices.

Misplaced as it was during Burleson's reign, greater efficiency led many of Burleson's latter-day predecessors to experiment with automobile service as early as 1899. That year's Annual Report of the Postmaster General stated: "In view of the prominence which these vehicles have recently attained in the development of the means of general transportation, it is believed that the time has come for utilizing them in connection with the carrying of the mails." The idea born in 1899 proved to be a viable one, beginning with the test of a small Winton "motor wagon," tried in Cleveland, Ohio, in December 1899. Cleveland was the home of the Winton Co.,

With the introduction of Parcel Post, carriers on motorcycle routes began having serious problems transporting mail.

then one of the nation's earliest quality automobile manufacturers. Alexander Winton, who had introduced his first gasoline-powered vehicles three years earlier, wanted nothing better than to demonstrate just how useful his motor vehicles were. Winton realized that the postal system was potentially a major client. The test covered a 22-mile route over paved and rough roads. Winton's vehicle completed the circuit in 147 minutes. The time required for a horse-drawn vehicle covering the same route was 360 minutes.

Farsighted postal officials realized that horse-drawn wagons were slow, especially in gridlock-plagued cities. They looked to automobiles as a way of overcoming slow service in congested areas. The general consensus was that "a motor (car) will stall no quicker than a horse." And, as for expense, which obviously varied depending upon the area of the country and the season just as the cost of feed for a horse and repairs for a wagon did, there was said to be good evidence that the cost of operating a motor vehicle was far less than the feeding and stabling of a horse. In light of these and similar findings, soon motor vehicles were being tested in

other cities, including: St. Louis, Missouri; Baltimore, Maryland; and Norfolk, Virginia.

Oddly enough, despite the fact that roads in urban areas tended to be better than in rural sections of the country, automobiles were not viewed any differently with respect to their possible use in conjunction with rural service. Managers within the Post Office Department grasped the significant advantages automobiles had over rural mail wagons, so much so that a rural automobile route was established in Adrian, Michigan, in 1902. Full government acceptance of automobiles for rural service came in 1906, when the Post Office Department formally granted permission for rural carriers to use automobiles following field tests in June and July over three routes outside of Washington, D.C.

Since only the type of vehicle being used changed, farm families initially applauded such innovation. They liked the fact that they could get faster service this way. They liked things until Albert Burleson took over as postmaster general.

By the time he assumed control of the Post Office Department in 1913, motor vehicles had become fairly popular with rural carriers. They were popular with Burleson, too. He needed little convincing concerning the value of motor vehicles. They figured prominently in his overall scheme for greatly improving postal efficiency. He expected to exploit them.

Where roads were good, and when the weather was dry, motor vehicles were effective in reducing collection and distribution times. There was no arguing that. And, like any good administrator interested in wringing every last drop of potential savings out of the mail system that he could, Burleson pushed for more and more motorized routes.

While by the close of 1915, rural motorized mail routes were declared "efficient and popular" by the Post Office Department, then Fourth Assistant Postmaster General James I. Blakslee stated that "The collection and delivery of mail on rural routes is undoubtedly greatly facilitated by improved highways and the use of motor vehicles." He was especially full of praise for automobiles, which he said "will give a powerful stimulus to the cause of good roads and improve the facilities available to our farming population for utilizing the parcel post system."

If motor vehicles allowed carriers to complete their routes faster than horse-drawn modes of transportation, the postal service, and not the carriers, was entitled to the savings, reasoned Burleson. From Burleson's point of view, one of the best ways to make the most of the anticipated savings was to replace as many wagon routes as possible with motorized routes, while at the same time consolidating two or more short horse-drawn routes into lengthened motorized routes. In this way, Burleson figured that he could get two routes covered for the price of one. He quickly proposed making horse-drawn routes 24 miles, while motorized routes were to cover about 50 miles.

When Burleson announced his plans to extend motorized routes, carriers, motorcycle makers, and postal patrons reacted violently. Ironically, this controversy would not have been quite so bad had the motorcycle manufacturers not drawn attention to the thrift, as was evident from their boastful ads that told of how carriers could finish their routes in an hour or two and then go fishing or to the circus. In this respect, the manufacturers largely brought this whole dilemma upon themselves. Such ads, and the resulting fallout, irked many carriers. It upset them because it gave the impression that they, as a class of public servants, only wanted to work the least amount to get by. W.H. James of Council Bluffs, Iowa, spoke for the majority of the carriers when he wrote an open letter to his colleagues, pub-

lished in *R.F.D. News*, stating that "The rural service means more than just rambling over a route and dropping the daily paper in the box and then trying to see how soon you can get back to the office .... It is time to slow down and do our utmost to be more efficient and give our patrons the best service possible."

The consolidation of many shorter routes into a few longer ones created chaos and exasperation. "The attempt to pile the work of four routes on three carriers, already overworked, is proving a monumental failure," stated one news story. Although postal officials calculated that each new 50-mile motorized route authorized in 1916 would consume eight hours, in reality these estimates were soon found to be unrealistic. Two motor routes were established in Georgia in March 1916. These were 54 and 52 miles long. The carriers, who were to be paid $1,800 annually, were to depart at 8:30 a.m. and return at 4:30 p.m. In short order the Madison, Georgia, *Madisonian*, reported that one carrier managed to finish his consolidated route during the first week by 10 p.m., the second week by 9 p.m., and finally found it lasted until 8 p.m. This was tantamount to forcing carriers to work both day and night shifts. Such conditions, said the newspaper, were sure to prompt the carrier to resign.

More often as not, the opposition was generally bipartisan in nature. A reader of the Centerville, (Iowa) *Daily Citizen*, was typical of those expressing outrage. "Democrats and Republicans alike are demanding redress in the rural mail service, and Mr.

Besides being able to accommodate large amounts of packages and letter mail, sidecars provided a major advantage in keeping mail dry.

Burleson must either come across with the goods (leaving things as they had been) or give way for someone who will." It was said that petitions and letters of protest from angry farmers, Granges, and other organizations poured into Washington.

Such reactions didn't phase Burleson much. This postal taskmaster had a tough hide. Morale meant nothing and neither did tenure. In his view, the system was grossly inefficient. He wanted to force postal employees to work longer and harder—and at no additional cost—and it was said that he particularly wanted its older workers to go in the process. It was further charged that he especially wanted to get rid of all old-time Republicans, which in the patronage-oriented postal system was somewhat true. Another claim was that he wanted to especially dump Union Army veterans, which was never really proven, although the unsympathetic press had a field day with that particular topic. The outrage was captured by the Baldwin City (Kansas) *Ledger,* which observed that Burleson's administration "recently attracted nationwide attention by the wholesale manner in which (it) decapitated clerks and carriers in the Washington (D.C.) post office who were found guilty of wearing the old bronze button and in connection therewith having given too many years of faithful service to Uncle Sam." According to the paper, "Protests from Grand Army of the Republic posts were of no avail, for their voting strength is not as great as it used to be and the South is strictly in the saddle." Carl D. Ruth, writing for the *Cleveland Leader,* expressed the view that "Responding heroically to the appeals of pie-hungry Democrats throughout the land, the Wilson administration is busily engaged pulling off one of the biggest patronage grabs in the history of national politics. Postmaster General Albert Sidney Burleson is the generalissimo and directing genius. His problem is so to reorganize the rural mail delivery system of the United States as to separate effectively and silently several thousand Republican mail carriers from the government payroll and substitute as many destitute but deserving Democrats."

Some argued that it wasn't so much a matter of how long one served or what party affiliation they held, as where they worked. Rural letter carriers were different from their city carrier counterparts, who received larger salaries and did not have to furnish or maintain vehicles. There also were inequities between rural carriers and postal clerks, who were said to work in "comfortable offices and are afforded convenient shelter from the vicissitudes and inclemencies of the season." Rural carriers had to render their service out in the open, regardless of weather or road conditions; a service in which three

or four hours is more than equal to seven or eight hours in comfortable offices.

Besides being despised by employees for his heavy-handed management style, Burleson was disliked for his efforts to set standards for almost everything, including mailboxes, workers' badges, postal locks, mail sacks, and postal vehicles.

One part of this move towards standardization included a push to create a standard type of small R.F.D. mail truck. This type of vehicle was a small screened truck with a minimum capacity of 80 cubic feet. The design was approved by Burleson in September 1915, but his action had no teeth. The design was simply passed along to each new motorized rural carrier as a suggestion. No particular make of chassis was specified, nor was there any compulsion to use the suggested body style. All the new carriers received was a blueprint. What was clear, though, was that the carrier was expected to pay for the new style truck. This kind of outlay was impossible on a rural carrier's meager wages. For this reason the idea was ignored. Rural carriers continued to use an assortment of wagons, carts, automobiles and motorcycles.

Burleson particularly disliked motorcycles. One objection had to do with the problems associated with having to juggle mailbags and parcels while maneuvering over country roads. This was a valid complaint. Because of their limited carrying capacity, motorcyclists frequently had to go back and forth to the post office two or three times to get all of the mail for their routes each day. Others chose to overload the cycles as much as possible. All sorts of bizarre bagging, bundling, and stacking techniques were concocted by carriers. Another reason why Burleson disliked cycles was that they afforded no real protection for the mail during foul weather. This, too, was valid. A third drawback was that they were considered to be more dangerous to operate than wagons or autos. Burleson used horror stories supplied by carriers to support his assertion that motorcycles were unsafe. Such stories were common. When carrier James Melton of Olustee, Oklahoma, ran over a dog, the head of the state's rural carriers association, Thomas Drew, dutifully reported the fact. This was the way he summed up the situation: "Result; motorcycle in the shop, Jim in bed and the dog dead." Drew obviously had a weird sense of humor because he added: "Rather expensive way to kill a dog!" The final reason why Burleson opposed motorcycles was because they allowed carriers to finish up too fast. He wanted every postal worker to do a full day's work for a full day's pay! It wasn't right, he thought, for someone to make as much in two or three hours as someone

By 1918, Parcel Post and the use of "postal cars" was a well-established fact of life on many rural routes. By then, nearly one-fifth of all rural letter carriers were using motor vehicles.

else that has to work six or more hours. If motorcycles were providing an unfair advantage, then they would have to go.

And so on July 24, 1915, Burleson issued an order prohibiting the use of motorcycles after January 1, 1916, on rural routes. This outraged the carriers that used motorcycles and inflamed the manufacturers. One Kentucky carrier who preferred to remain anonymous, thought that the postmaster general had gone way too far. "If a carrier is willing to buy a more expensive rig, whether it is an auto, traction line, motorcycle or railroad train, and gets the Department's consent to use same, then should he or should he not be paid a full day's wage for covering a 24-mile route?"

For their part, the motorcycle manufacturers gathered in Detroit to map out a strategy for overriding Burleson's ban. This resulted in the creation of a lobbying campaign in Congress to back the use of motorcycles equipped with sidevans. That, in effect, transformed the two-wheelers into tricars, which was something Burleson hadn't objected to.

The ban also made little sense financially. As of January 1, there was about $2 million worth of motorcycles in use throughout the country moving rural mail.

No one doubted that the postmaster general could require carriers to furnish their own vehicles. That had been the way things had been since the start of R.F.D. What was at issue was whether he could ban a specific type of vehicle. To the carriers' way of thinking they believed that they would certainly be the first to realize if one particular mode of transportation was inadequate, but Burleson believed that he was a much better judge of that than they were.

Perhaps Burleson's biggest mistake was that he appears to have underestimated the opposition. He expected them to knuckle under without much of a fight, but he was woefully mistaken. Rural carriers were thoroughly organized by 1915. They had good friends in congress. They had grown to be a factor to be reckoned with in politics. Noted one commentator in 1915, "The Congressman whose heart does not bleed for the rural carrier at each executive order is the exception." The perception was that the letter carriers' enmity was dreaded by the average Congressman more than that of some of the leading local and national politicians.

Much to Burleson's disappointment, in the summer of 1915 Congress weighed in of the subject. Included in the conference report on the Post Office Department's appropriation was a provision that read: "The Postmaster General in his discretion may require all carriers to furnish sufficient equipment to properly handle postal business on their routes." While this was clearly considered "vague language," some in Congress believed that the particular offending paragraph could be taken to prohibit the use of all motor vehicles, including motorcycles.

This idea caught Burleson totally off-guard. He had always wanted to encourage greater use of automobiles and trucks on rural routes because they could serve more families and faster than horse-drawn routes could. He envisioned this as an enticement to local communities to upgrade their roads so that they could obtain motorized routes. He never wanted an overall ban on all motor vehicles. The only thing he wanted to do was stop the use of motorcycles. The conference report went too far!

In the summer of 1915, rural carriers asked key members of Congress to clarify the language of report. Senator Charles E. Townsend, the ranking Republican minority member of the Senate Post Office Committee, was empathetic. "I do not believe there can be any misunderstanding as to the intent of the Congress," he said. "The Postmaster General should not prohibit the use of any motor vehicles, and this, of course, includes motorcycles upon rural routes if such vehicles were adequate for the proper delivery of the mail." But Townsend went further. The Michigan Senator drew a figurative line in the sand when he told his colleagues: "There has not been harmony between the Congress and the Post Office Department, and of late this has come to a point where, to me, it seems as though the Senate of the United States must take its stand and insist that its legally expressed will shall be observed."

Under pressure from the manufacturers and members of Congress, on October 2, 1915, Burleson caved in. He amended the order prohibiting the use of motorcycles, provided they included side bodies. In keeping with his obsession to standardize every facet of postal operations, Burleson issued exacting specifications for such acceptable sidecars. The required body size was to be 42 inches

long, 24 inches wide, and 18 inches high. The whole thing was to protect the mail thoroughly from damage and loss. Motorcycle makers quickly began selling sidecars that conformed with these specifications. Priced at about $200, these could accommodate about 50 pounds of mail.

The president of the Motorcycle Manufacturers Association, T.W. Henderson, immediately claimed victory. "The Committee which I appointed to wait on the Postmaster General, consisting of George M. Hendee, Ignaz Schwinn, Walter Davidson and Jesse Edwards, have been successful in inducing him to modify his order ...."

Burleson's initial decree infuriated those carriers who were using motorcycles, but many complied, selling their motorcycles in order to purchase a wagon or automobile. These same carriers were livid when Burleson reversed himself, as he did within a matter of weeks. D.A. Pickell of Huron, South Dakota, was one of those caught off-guard by Burleson's change of heart. In January 1916, he wrote: "When Postmaster General Burleson passed the order prohibiting the use of motorcycles after January 1, I began looking for a place to dispose of mine as I could not afford to keep it until after spring, thinking I would not be able to use it. I found a buyer and sold (it) for cash and I have been sorry for it ever since." Other carriers would be doubly angry when Burleson flip-flopped again. In 1916, he softened his stance even more, allowing motorcycles without sidecars to be used.

This further reversal prompted the Hendee Manufacturing Co., maker of the Indian motorcycle, to boast, "Now that the ban on motorcycles for R.F.D. Service has been lifted, there is offered unlimited opportunity for R.F.D. men to increase their earnings. Motorcycles, with or without (a) parcel car, may now be used on any horse-drawn route! The delivery of mail is squarely up to the carrier without restriction as to the form of vehicle he shall or shall not use. Hundreds of R.F.D. men throughout the country are making their routes really pay by using the Indian motorcycle." Harley-Davidson did about the same thing, using a two-page advertisement in *R.F.D. News*, published in August 5, 1916, to proclaim, "The order forbidding the use, by rural carriers, of motorcycles without sidevans has been changed. This means that you can use a motorcycle with or without sidecar or side van."

CITY DELIVERY VEHICLES

USA
Chapter *1*

These two "Parcel Post Delivery" trucks were used in Erie, Pennsylvania. (Photograph courtesy of the United States Postal Service)

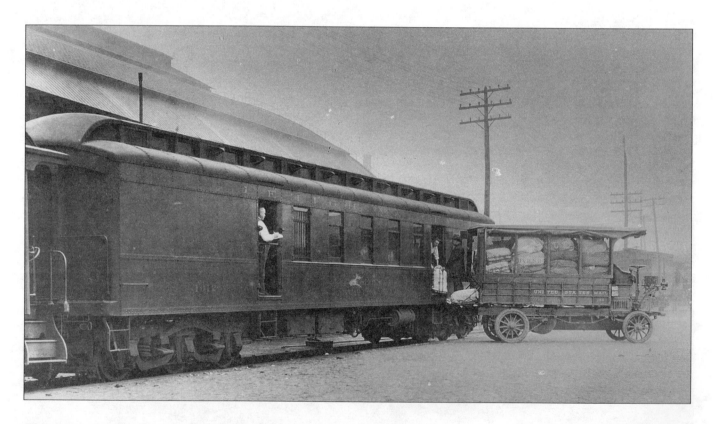

This particular model screen truck was the perfect height for making pick-ups from railway mail cars. (Photograph courtesy of the United States Postal Service)

An idea in 1899 to provide motorized mail service in Cleveland, Ohio, spawned the birth of the postal service motor vehicle fleet in December of that year. Cleveland was the home of the Winton Co., then one of the nation's earliest quality automobile manufacturers. Alexander Winton, who had introduced his first gasoline-powered vehicles three years earlier, wanted nothing more than to demonstrate just how useful his motor vehicles were. Winton realized that the Post Office Department was a potential major customer. The test of this 1899 vehicle covered a 22-mile route over paved and rough roads. Winton's vehicle completed the circuit in 147 minutes. The time required for a horse-drawn vehicle to cover the same route was 360 minutes. Farsighted postal officials realized that horse-drawn wagons were slow, especially in gridlock-prone cities. They looked to automobiles as a way of overcoming slow city service. The general consensus was that "a motor (car) will stall no quicker than a horse." And, as for expense, which obviously varied depending upon the area of the country and the season of the year, from this test it was clear enough that there was good evidence that the cost of operating a motor vehicle was far less than that for feeding and stabling a horse.

In February 1904, the postmaster of St. Louis asked postal service headquarters for permission to dispose of two outmoded horse-drawn "Collection and Distribution Wagons" and to replace them with a motorized light delivery van in advance of the upcoming World's Fair. According to the Postal Service's photographic archives, this Knox waterless mail van was used at the St. Louis Exposition in 1904. It was powered by a single-cylinder, six-hp engine that could haul up to 1,000 pounds of mail. (Photograph courtesy of the United States Postal Service)

Two "Columbia" Model Mark 43 autocars were used in Baltimore, Maryland, in 1906 to test the feasibility of collecting mail in the commercial districts of the city. These were basically ordinary touring cars, with the rear portion removed and a specially designed body mounted on each chassis in back of the front seat. The machines were equipped with two horizontally opposed two-cylinder engines that had 12- to 14-hp ratings. This test was a major success, one which convinced postal officials of the value of motor vehicles. The top view shows a front and rear view of the pair, while the bottom view shows one of the vehicles loaded down with mailbags. This was produced for illustrative purposes at the Baltimore post office to show that an automobile could transport as much mail as a small mail wagon if necessary. This much mail was never transported at one time.

This 1906 Model F White steam truck was used in Boston, Massachusetts.

This Oldsmobile screen-body express wagon was used in Detroit in the summer of 1906 to transport mail between the main post office and Station F (located at the intersection of Lyman Place and Russell Street). Four trips were made on Sundays, six on Saturdays and seven on all other days. Typically it took about 20 minutes to cover the nine-mile round trip distance. Gasoline consumption on this Oldsmobile averaged about 11 miles per gallon. The red, white, and blue vehicle, with red running gear, was operated under contract to the city post office by the Auto-Express Co.

The postmaster of Milwaukee, Wisconsin, arranged for three steam-powered vehicles to be tested in 1907. These Johnson Service Co. cars were the first postal automobiles equipped with specially constructed bodies. The vehicles were manufactured in Milwaukee and furnished under contract to the post office at a rate of $3,500 each per annum. They were propelled by four-cylinder, 30-hp, steam engines. Kerosene was used as fuel. These were heavy vehicles. The running weight of each of these mail cars was 3,100 pounds.

In conjunction with the 1907 Jamestown Exposition, the Post Office Department employed two Waltham Manufacturing Co. "Orient Surreys" with screen-sides. One of these single-cylinder, four-hp motor wagons was used to carry mail between the temporary Exposition post office and the Norfolk, Virginia, post office. The other hauled mail between the Exposition's post office and the steamship docks at Pine Beach, Virginia.

One of five Brush "package carts" used in Washington, D.C., in 1908, this vehicle shows significant signs of wear and tear. The front and rear fenders are gone, as is the fresh paint on the front axle. The power for this 950-pound vehicle was provided by a single-cylinder, six-hp Cadillac engine. Alanson P. Brush preferred to use wood in his vehicles whenever possible. He made axles and chassis out of wood because of its light weight and low cost. He favored wood over steel, believing that the metal would fracture under repeated stress. (Photograph courtesy of Thomas E. Stanton)

Years before the Post Office Department routinely began assigning government motor vehicles to letter carriers, George L. Baum decided to use his own car on his Washington, D.C., route. The box body was homemade by Baum. This photograph, taken in December 1918, shows Baum collecting midday mail.

Talks between representatives from the Office of the Fourth Assistant Postmaster General and the Overland Automobile Co. late in 1908 led to the use of two Overlands in Indianapolis, Indiana, in 1909. The vehicles were used 10 hours a day, principally in residential districts, for collections from letter boxes. One of the two Indianapolis Overlands was driven by E.R. Miller, shown here in 1909. Reminiscing in 1957, Miller, then residing in Sevier, Utah, recalled how mail trucks back then had the right of way over everything else on the road.

In 1909, the postmaster of Philadelphia, Pennsylvania, began using four Autocar trucks for package collection in outlying suburbs. These four vehicles did the work of nine horse-drawn mail wagons and they were able to cover twice the territory. On average, each of these four trucks made between 120 and 150 stops per day.

According to Postal Service photographic archives, this 1911 screen-body "Auto Wagon" was one of the first International Harvesters purchased by the postal system. (Photograph courtesy of the United States Postal Service)

In 1911, the Post Office Department tested "drop bottom" mailboxes in 20 cities, including Milwaukee, Wisconsin, where this half-ton Johnson Service Co. "light delivery wagon" was used for collections. The Milwaukee-made vehicle was powered by a four-cylinder, 35-hp gasoline engine. The idea for drop bottom boxes came from David C. Owens, Milwaukee's postmaster. "The idea appealed to me," Owens said, "when I first became postmaster and being formerly in the coal business, where drop bottom cars have become generally used, I thought the same principle could be applied to the mailbox. In this way, the carrier can empty a dozen or more boxes in the same time as he could empty one by the old method of reaching in and hauling the mail out by hand." This type of box was basically the same as the others then in use, except that instead of removing mail from the front or side, these had a hinged bottom that would automatically dump all the contents into the carrier's sack as soon as it was unlocked. The first 500 drop bottom boxes were manufactured in Milwaukee by the A.O. Smith Co.

The postmaster of Detroit didn't have far to go to find this 1912 Abbott-Detroit. It was built in his hometown. Although the exact number of Abbott-Detroits used in Detroit is unclear, according to an article in the April 1912 issue of The Commercial Vehicle, the service provided was "very satisfactory to both government officials and its maker."

This one-ton chain-drive Lauth-Juergens Motor Car Co. truck was used in Toledo, Ohio, in 1912. (Photograph courtesy of the United States Postal Service)

A Model T Ford "C-cab" delivery van was used in 1912 in Gardner, Massachusetts. It featured nice touches such as a wooden body, speedometer, dual six-inch gas headlamps, three oil lamps, and "lipped" front fenders.

The Post Office Department purchased 31 Garfords in 1912. According to the elated manufacturer, this "is probably one of the largest individual orders for commercial cars ever placed." This particular Garford, towing a Sechler "Trailmobile," made a 663-mile mail run from its factory in Lima, Ohio, to Washington, D.C., in 1918 to prove that improved highways and the speed of the postal service went hand in hand. Sechler trailers were commonly attached to large trucks and postal streetcars when mail volumes were particularly high.

Several half-ton Studebaker "20" panel delivery trucks were provided under contract to the Pittsburgh post office for use in 1913 in connection with Parcel Post Service. According to one Pittsburgh newspaper, the fact that the trucks were not government owned was "typical of the Government's conservatism." It eliminated the need for postal mechanics and repair facilities, while affording time to study the value of motor trucks. In this particular case, the delivery wagons that were provided were the product of two divisions of the Studebaker Corp. These $800 trucks combined a Studebaker body with a Flanders chassis. Although the resulting truck was billed as "everything a delivery car ought to be," the body was its greatest selling point. The body was finely constructed and handsomely finished in deep green with a cream colored side panel. These trucks were equipped with four-cylinder engines that developed about 20 hp.

The Post Office Department ordered a sizable number of Autocar's 1913 "Parcel Post Motor Truck" with side-entry step-up bodies. Autocars were short, with a 97-inch wheelbase, but they could haul up to two tons. Its compact size gave it a turning radius of about 17 feet. This allowed the vehicle to navigate into tight spaces and through crowded streets. The engine was located under the driver's compartment to save space. Because of this, and other features, the manufacturer boasted that "Every possible inch is used to carry the paying load." One disadvantage with this body style was its height, a feature that made it somewhat difficult to load and unload from the rear.

Ten three-quarter-ton Lippard-Stewart "delivery cars" with wire-side express bodies were used for Parcel Post Service in Washington, D.C., in 1913. These featured a sloping Renault-style hood with the radiator immediately in front of the driver. One of the novel features of these vehicles was the inclusion of an "automatic speed governor," a device that the truckmaker claimed provided "an absolute protection against foolish waste of power and ignorant driving." Manufactured by the Lippard-Stewart Motor Car Co. of Buffalo, New York, these were "assembled trucks." That means that they were put together largely with an array of parts from other respected manufacturers. For example, the engines were from Continental, the transmissions were from Brown-Lipe, the axles and bearings were from Timken, and the magnetos were from Eisemann.

Screen-side vehicles, such as these 1914 Whites, were widely used in large cities throughout the country to transport mail between postal facilities. In this case, the heavy-gauge metal screening is obscured by the canvas curtains that helped protect the mail from moisture. The screen-body style was modeled after a type of postal wagon that was introduced in Sherman, Texas, in 1886. Prior to that, mail wagons typically had canvas sides that could easily be sliced open. Thousands of these horse-drawn "Screen Wagons" were in use along with trucks. Some of these mail wagons survived into the 1950s. (Photograph courtesy of George Shifflet)

These two different models of Buick screen-side trucks were used in Paterson, New Jersey, in 1914 in conjunction with Parcel Post Service. (Photograph courtesy of the United States Postal Service)

Based in York, Pennsylvania, the Hoover Wagon Co. was a highly respected manufacturer of postal vehicle bodies during the first two decades of this century. It also briefly manufactured light-duty trucks, such as this screen-side Parcel Post truck. (Photograph courtesy of the United States Postal Service)

Heavy-duty Riker trucks from Locomobile of Bridgeport, Connecticut, could accommodate massive quantities of mail, especially during the Christmas rush.

By the summer of 1913, the Post Office Department was equipping its Parcel Post trucks with fixed or sliding interior shelves. These typically ran the full width of the body and facilitated stacking packages without crushing those on the bottom.

The Post Office Department pampered its fledgling fleet. Vehicle operators, such as the drivers of these 1914 White trucks in Minneapolis, Minnesota, were under strict orders, with severe penalties for any misuse. These included: permitting someone else to operate the vehicle without authorization — 100 demerits; allowing an unauthorized passenger aboard — 100 to 500 demerits; stopping with the left side to the curb — 50 demerits; calling out a repairman when nothing was wrong or when some slight adjustment could have corrected the problem — 10 demerits; driving over rough places and causing a breakdown — 20 to 200 demerits; failing to check the oil before leaving the garage — 50 to 200 demerits; damaging the tires through negligence — 25 to 500 demerits; and driving too fast — 10 to 200 demerits. Among the other rules that were to be observed was "the chauffeur who takes out a motor truck at the commencement of the day's run must examine the gasoline tank to see that it is full and that the radiator has been supplied with water, and all parts are properly lubricated, and that the brakes, horn, and lamps are in good working order. Furthermore, the "day" driver was to make sure that the headlamps were full of oil and in working order prior to turning the truck over to the "night" man.

Acceptable operating speeds were far lower than they are today. In Chicago, where this Model T Ford was driven by Albert Pieper, Jr., the maximum safe speed allowed by the Post Office Department for a major boulevard was 12 miles per hour, while on most other city streets, speeds were restricted to half that amount. To further reduce the risk of speeding, in 1923 the postal service installed governors in all of its 4,447 motor vehicles. (Photograph courtesy of the family of Albert Pieper, Jr.)

Because the Post Office Department was perfectly satisfied with its 1904 horse-drawn screen wagon specifications, when it came time to order bodies for its mail trucks it insisted on having the same wagon-style bodies mounted onto automotive frames. This was fine with many of the early car companies, especially those that were formally wagon makers. The screen-bodies on these trucks, shown neatly parked inside a Post Office Department garage, are nearly identical to those used on horse-drawn screen wagons from 1904 up through the 1950s. (Photograph courtesy of the United States Postal Service)

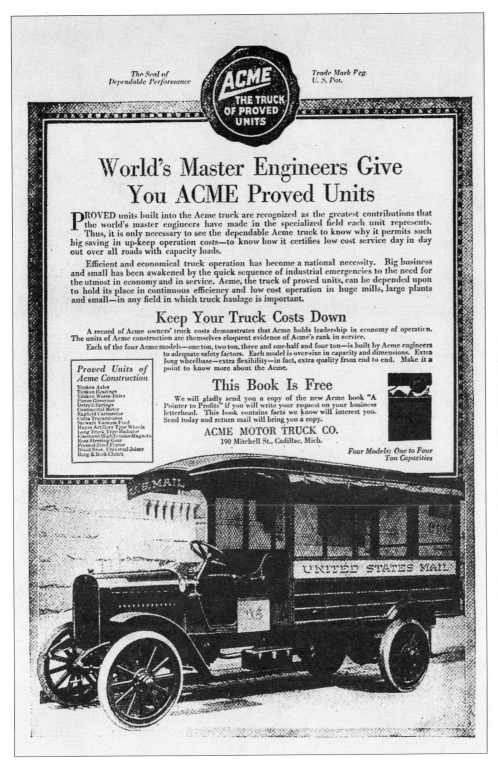

The Acme Motor Truck Co. was proud of the fact that its trucks were assembled from other companies' parts. It claimed that the inclusion of such "Proved units built into the Acme truck are recognized as the greatest contributions that the world's master engineers have made in the specialized field each unit represents;" and Acme certainly had enough of them built into each truck. Among the "proved units" that were used were Timken axles and bearings, Pierce governors, Detroit springs, Continental engines, Rayfield carburetors, Cotta transmissions, Stewart vacuum feeds, Hayes artillery-type wheels, Eisemann high tension magnetos, Blood Brothers universal joints, and Borg and Beck clutches. What was missing from these trucks were creature comforts, such as an enclosed cab, windshield, windshield wipers, and electric headlamps.

Thirty-three Denby Motor Truck Co. three-quarter-ton screen-body trucks were sold to New York City contractors working for the Post Office Department (top). The bottom view provides a closer look at one of the 33 vehicles. Denby began manufacturing typically large-sized vehicles in 1914. It did not survive the Great Depression. (Photographs courtesy of the United States Postal Service)

New White Motor Co. trucks, such as this one photographed in front of the Washington, D.C., post office in 1914, were often delivered to the postal service in rather stripped-down fashion. They typically were delivered without a spare tire and tube. These items were purchased separately.

Limited with respect to its lamping, this three-quarter-ton White Motor Co. screen-body mail truck was obviously better equipped for daytime driving. (Photograph courtesy of the United States Postal Service)

This Model L "VIM" one-ton mail truck manufactured by the Touraine Co. of Philadelphia, Pennsylvania, was used in Norfolk, Virginia. It featured a 20-hp, four-cylinder engine and three-speed transmission. Its body was sheet metal with spot welded construction. The base price of this style of truck was $635. Although the company boasted of becoming "in less than a year the second largest producers of commercial cars in America," comparatively few VIM mail trucks were actually used. (Photograph courtesy of the United States Postal Service)

Featuring a Renault-style hood, this 1916 one-ton Krebs had little going for it. It was somewhat underpowered for its size, with its 22-hp engine. It also was nearly void of creature comforts. The cab was totally open, lacking even a windshield. Electric lights also were not provided. This was the first year that the Post Office Department used Krebs trucks.

Heavy-duty Packards, such as this vintage 1916 2,000-pound "ID" truck chassis with enclosed cab and screen-body, were popular mail trucks. (Photograph courtesy of the United States Postal Service)

Of the 295 mail trucks used in Chicago in 1916, three-quarter-ton Fords were principally used for Parcel Post Service and letter box collections, while Packards and White trucks were used to haul heavier loads between substations, the main post office and railway depots. The Packards and Whites were one-and-one-half-ton to three-ton types. This is an example of the one-and-one-half-ton screen-body Packards that were used. The drivers of the three-ton trucks were accompanied by a laborer who assisted in off-loading pouches and sacks. Leather and canvas pouches typically contained 35 pounds of mail. Tie-sacks, on the other hand, usually held 65 pounds. The times allowed for loading and unloading mail trucks were based on the weight of the load and the capacity of the truck. (Photograph courtesy of the United States Postal Service)

The builder of medium- and heavy-duty trucks between 1905 and 1923, the Packard Motor Car Co. produced this one-and-one-half-ton screen-side truck shortly before World War I. At that time, and after the war too, the Post Office Department had a preference for solid rubber tires. An extensive study was conducted by postal engineers that supported the use of solid over pneumatic tires. Postal engineers considered inflatable tires to be too dangerous, too flimsy, too prone to blowouts, and too likely to be stolen. (Photograph courtesy of the United States Postal Service)

Heavy-duty postal trucks, such as these three-ton Federal Motor Truck Co. units used in Minneapolis, Minnesota, were used as much as 10 to 18 hours a day. To maximize their use, frequently two or more drivers were assigned to each vehicle so that they could be kept in continuous service. Such trucks were scheduled to meet inbound railway mail trains at the various depots around town so that the mail cars could be promptly unloaded. Most towns had more than one depot. Chicago was typical of many of the nation's larger cities. It had six railway stations and five railway terminals in 1916.

The Secretary of War approved the transfer of 5,778 surplus trucks to the Post Office Department following World War I. Trucks such as these 1917 Reo Model F three-quarter-tons with covered flareboard express bodies were placed in rented warehouses until they could be used. The annual cost of the storage amounted to about $12 per truck. Many of these second-hand trucks were never needed after years of storage.

Federal Motor Truck Co. trucks, such as this model with its roll-down storm curtains, canopy top express body and large searchlight, were used to help promote the creation of improved highways in rural and urban areas. Such illustrations highlighted the Post Office Department's growing reliance on motor vehicles. Views such as this implied the promise that better roads would yield better service. Fourth Assistant Postmaster General James I. Blakslee hammered home this connection when he observed in 1918 that "Nine-tenths (of all rural roads) begin and end nowhere." This was being overcome he said, with the postal system's attempt "in a small way to function or utilize the improved highways ... in such a manner as will enlarge the means of communication, increase the avenue of conveyance and ultimately bring the original producer into as nearly direct contact with the ultimate consumer as is possible." This particular Federal truck was used in Baltimore, Maryland. (Photograph courtesy of the United States Postal Service)

During the First World War the Army Post Office used a variety of vehicles to move military mail in Europe. Some of these were heavy-duty trucks of foreign manufacture, while others were American-made brutes. Those made in America were dubbed "USA" or "Liberty" trucks. Nearly 9,500 of these standardized "B" class vehicles were produced for the U.S. military during World War I by 15 different truckmakers. After the war these trucks, and tens of thousands of smaller sizes, were offered to the Post Office Department. The plan was to use the one-ton or smaller surplus vehicles on rural mail routes, while the one-and-one-half-ton to three-ton trucks were to be used for longer hauls between major cities or for City Delivery Service. Neither of these plans ever really materialized. The massive "Liberty" trucks weren't highly adaptable to the needs of the postal service. Automotive engineers and postal officials realized that these were grossly overpowered and too heavy for economical operations in ordinary commercial service.

Besides being offered hand-me-down military surplus, the Post Office Department acquired its own new vehicles during the war years, such as these White screen-side trucks. (Photograph courtesy of the Library of Congress)

Post Office Department's specifications for three-ton trucks, such as this one that provided "South Shore Service" between Minneapolis and Lake Minnetonka, Minnesota, called for the frame of the body to be crafted of oak or white ash, while the body panels were to be of the best grade of thoroughly seasoned and air-dried poplar. The specifications for this size truck were originally drawn in March 1919. Further revisions of the specifications were made in February 1920 and May 1922. (Photograph courtesy of the United States Postal Service)

In 1918, the Post Office Department had a mixed bag of over 560 government-owned mail trucks ranging in size from half-tons to four-tons. The bulk of the larger trucks were used in major urban areas. The lighter weights were mostly Model T Fords that were used throughout the country. Makes included 268 Fords, 135 Whites, 70 GMCs, 37 Studebakers, 13 Packards, five Buicks, and a few vehicles from other assorted manufacturers. As these photographs illustrate, the Model T Ford body styles varied. (Photographs courtesy of the United States Postal Service)

Manufactured in Cincinnati, Ohio, by United States Motor Truck, this heavily loaded truck was used in Buffalo, New York.

Built in Detroit, Michigan, this one-ton chain-driven Signal Motor Truck Co. rig had a base price of $1,400, $100 less than a comparable worm drive version. This is an ideal example of an "assembled truck," pieced together using components furnished by an array of different manufacturers. In this particular case, the truck consisted of Timken axles and bearings, a Continental engine, Covert transmission, Gemmer steering gear, Eisemann magneto, and Stromberg carburetor. The fact that a truck was manufactured from assembled parts wasn't necessarily a bad thing. Most of the components had proven track records for reliability, probably far greater than any parts that might have been produced by the truck company itself.

Although GMC originally furnished three-quarter-ton trucks such as this with pneumatic tires, the postal service preferred to use solid tires whenever possible. Postal officials weren't alone. Pneumatic tires did not become popular among large truck users until the late 1920s. The increased use of pneumatic tires was applauded by highway departments around the country because they were less destructive to road surfaces. (Photograph courtesy of the United States Postal Service)

What is interesting about this pair of White screen-side mail trucks is their resilient "airless" type tires. Somewhat common in the mid-1920s, this style of tire was something of a halfway measure between the hard ride of solid rubber tires and the cushioned ride provided by pneumatic tires.

This one-ton Chevrolet utility express truck with screen-body was used in 1924. The chassis featured a 120-inch wheelbase. Power was provided by an inline four-cylinder engine capable of developing about 35 hp.

Besides the trucks that were furnished under short-term contracts to the postal service, when the Post Office Department established its own Motor Vehicle Service on July 1, 1915, it owned outright only 32 mail trucks. These were divided among the nation's five largest cities. Over the next five years the Motor Vehicle Service added nearly 2,500 more motor vehicles and extended service to 134 cities. By 1924, the government's postal fleet had grown to include 5,290 government-owned trucks. By that time, mail trucks were being operated in 486 cities. This one-ton Graham Brothers screen-side mail truck joined the fleet that year. (Photograph courtesy of Dr. John Weimer)

Greatly respected for their durability and reliability, and a proven workhorse, Mack AC stake body trucks such as this often stayed in service well beyond their prime. It was not uncommon to find hand-cranked, chain-driven, solid-rubber tired Mack trucks still hauling mail three and four decades after rolling off the manufacturer's Allentown, Pennsylvania, assembly line. With a top speed of about 15 miles per hour, they were like lumbering dinosaurs. Three were reassigned from Washington, D.C., to Philadelphia in the 1950s, but, according to George Shifflet, one of the postal workers involved in the transfer, "They took forever at that speed getting there."

This photograph, taken in 1933, probably shows this Mack AC screen-side truck used in Norfolk, Virginia, at the prime of its life. Many World War I vintage Macks remained in service well into the 1950s. (Photograph courtesy of Jacob Cheeks, Postmaster of Norfolk, Virginia)

A great deal of tender loving care was needed to keep this 1928 three-ton International Harvester Model HS-54 on the road. The "HS" designation indicated that it was powered by a Hall-Scott engine. This particular photograph was taken in the mid-1940s at the Baltimore, Maryland, post office garage. One of the distinguishing features of International trucks produced during the 1920s was the placement of the headlamps back on the cowling behind the fenders. (Photograph courtesy of the United States Postal Service)

Spare tires typically were not furnished when new mail trucks, such as this White, came from the factory. Spares were purchased separately by the Post Office Department.

Chevrolet furnished a small number of 1929 Model AD chassis to the Post Office Department during the Great Depression (top photograph). These were fitted with wooden bodies for one-and-one-half-ton trucks manufactured by separate companies. This body style matches those used on Model AA Ford chassis (bottom). (Left photograph courtesy of George Shifflet)

Praised for its shapely contours and stylish detailing, traits apparent in these two sizes of Model D mail trucks, the D-series was introduced by International Harvester in 1937. Production of the D-line of trucks continued until World War II. (Photographs courtesy of the United States Postal Service)

Seven new 1937 three-quarter-ton Model D-15 cabs with special Parcel Post mail truck bodies were placed on display outside the main Washington, D.C., post office on Capitol Hill shortly after being delivered by International Harvester. This building now houses the Smithsonian Institution's National Postal Museum. (Photograph courtesy of the United States Postal Service)

According to Larry Clark, truck number "18351 was the best maintained truck in the fleet." That was hard to believe, judging from this 1941 view of Clark's battered 1931 Model AA Ford. With America's entry into World War II, replacement vehicles became nearly impossible to acquire. Almost every new motor vehicle was devoted to the war effort. By 1945, approximately 90 percent of all postal vehicles were obsolete, many having been on the road since the 1920s and 1930s. Ford mail trucks purchased in the early 1930s included wooden bodies crafted by such firms as the Mifflinburg Body Co. (Mifflinburg, Pennsylvania) and the Metropolitan Body Corp. (Bridgeport, Connecticut). (Photograph courtesy of the National Association of Letter Carriers)

To augment its 10-year-old fleet of Model A Fords, the Post Office Department purchased a limited number of 1941 Ford three-quarter-ton chassis. These were fitted out with different bodies including this type, which was fabricated by Gerstenslager of Wooster, Ohio. Gerstenslager was a major producer of post office truck bodies, building about 25,000 between 1949 and 1963.

Prior to and during World War II, no money was appropriated for new mail trucks. This bothered Jesse Donaldson, Harry Truman's second Postmaster General, who observed, "During World War II we were in the basement so far as priority was concerned and (the postal service) could obtain no equipment." During the Truman Administration an ambitious plan was initiated to replace all mail trucks purchased before 1947. This initial plan was delayed due to the ever increasing volume of mail, which grew from 36 billion pieces in 1947 to nearly 50 billion by 1950. Instead, the phase-out was stretched over six years. This allowed the Post Office Department to gradually retire trucks in installments. Under this plan, it replaced 1,820 trucks in 1947; 1,720 in 1948; 1,771 in 1949; 3,050 in 1950; 5,227 in 1951; and 5,925 in 1952. This was an expensive proposition. By 1950, the postal service was paying 100 percent more for trucks than it did before World War II. Among the replacements was this one-ton Ford Model F-3 truck added to the postal service's fleet in 1949-1950 largely as replacements for the aging Model A Fords purchased in the late 1920s and early 1930s.

Postal officials from Chicago and Detroit were on-hand to inspect the first Dodge B-1 Series mail trucks to come off the assembly line in 1948.

By the mid-1950s, postal officials considered vehicles such as this 1948 International Harvester one-and-one-half-ton Model KB-5 to be overweight and cumbersome. They also hated the fact that it had double rear tires. As part of their long-range vehicle planning program that was designed to phase out all pre-1950s vehicles, postal officials opted to replace the KB-5s with Chevrolet forward control vans. Such vans afforded up to a third more capacity, weighed half as much, offered better visibility, were right-hand drive, and were easier to maneuver.

This 1948 three-ton White was purchased at the wrong time. Within a matter of years, this style of truck was being replaced by forward control vans with about the same capacity.

Forward control step vans were not part of the postal service's fleet before 1949. That year Ford introduced two sizes of its F-3 parcel delivery chassis — a 104- or a 122-inch wheelbase. Ford furnished the front windshield portion and chassis to the Boyertown Auto Body Works in Boyertown, Pennsylvania. Boyertown fabricated the remainder of the shell. This first generation forward control mail van, which carried a nominal three-quarter-ton heavy-duty truck rating, served in many ways as the prototype for the thousands of subsequent vans from Ford and other manufacturers that were acquired by the postal system after 1949.

A large number of the 2,125 Dodge B-3-G two-ton trucks acquired in 1952 were assigned to New York City. The Post Office Department purchased these 114-hp trucks for $2,469.82 each. (Photograph courtesy of Joseph H. Cohen, United States Postal Service, New York City)

What with the Korean War, labor unrest, and material shortages, the debut of International Harvester's "L" series in 1950 probably could not have come at a worse time. The steel body on this heavy-duty L-185 mail truck was both a blessing and a curse. It was strong and easy to repair when it was new, but in later years it was prone to rusting out. This is one reason why so few of this type of Truman-era truck have survived.

One of 3,750 one-ton Dodge B-2-Ds acquired in 1951, this particular truck was one of a small number that was used a few years later in conjunction with a "Sav-a-Day with Speedi-Way" service. This novel local initiative, inaugurated in St. Louis, Missouri, in 1958 was designed to encourage businesses to mail earlier in the day, thereby alleviating the impact of the evening mail rush. These specially designated 103-hp Dodges, dubbed "Speedi collection trucks," made extra pickups between 11:30 a.m. and 1 p.m. from major mailers, as well as from 85 mailboxes located in St. Louis's central business district.

Two-thousand one-ton Dodge B-3-Ds were purchased in 1952. These trucks featured a 103-hp engine and a price tag of $1,762.02 each. (Photograph courtesy of the Library of Congress)

The Post Office Department acquired 1,800 half-ton Dodge B-3-Bs in 1952, including the five shown here. The price of the 97-hp B-3-Bs was $1,330.27 each. (Photograph courtesy of the United States Postal Service)

Based on 1953 and 1954 experiments, the Post Office Department began to seriously consider "jeeps." In 1954, this Willys Motors postal jeep was tested. The origin of the name remains a mystery. Some believe that it was derived from its early military vehicle abbreviation — "G.P." (General Purpose) — while others attribute it to the name of a Popeye comic strip character — Eugene the Jeep. Based upon the success of these early trials, additional CJ-3s were purchased in 1955.

In a head-to-head contest with an innovative Marco van in 1954, this three-quarter-ton forward control Twin Coach won out. The Twin Coach had conventional rear-wheel drive, sliding doors with drop-down windows, and an independent suspension composed of Nash passenger car parts. The engine was a four-cycle, 60-hp Continental. The transmission was a three-speed automatic furnished by Detroit. The body, roof, and side panels reportedly were made from existing International Harvester stampings. As a result of the 1950s testing program, 3,791 "sit-or-stand" mini-vans were placed in service in 1955 as part of the nation's City Delivery Service.

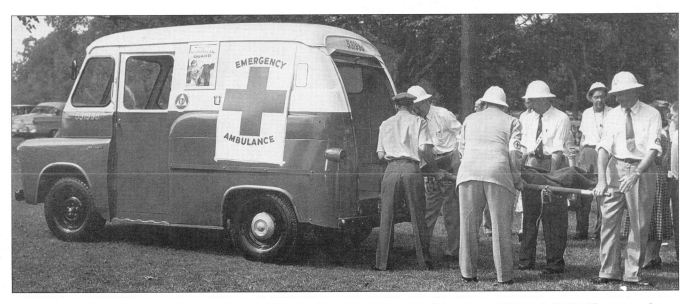

Three-thousand right-hand drive Dodge C-3-C6 mail vans were acquired between 1955 and 1957. These purchases amounted to about $6.2 million. These vehicles were powered by 115-hp engines and were rated with a three-quarter-ton capacity. In the event of a national emergency, postal vehicles could be used for Civil Defense. In this case, a Dodge C-3-C6 was used as an ambulance during a mock emergency exercise in Washington, D.C. The arrival of another of these vans at Minden, Louisiana, in 1957 prompted the postmaster to write this birth announcement-like memorandum to the regional manager for vehicle service:

Well, she arrived about 7:30 in the morning. She is beautifully formed and percolates freely. She caused quite a stir among the local clientele of the post office. Such a short, chunky little darling she is. Her breathing is perfect and her Red, White and Blue coloring would stand out anywhere. We are indeed proud of the newest addition to the Minden, Louisiana, post office, so pleased that we had her picture made for the local paper. We are casting about in our minds for a suitable name for her, because we hope to have her around for quite a spell. Now we are looking forward to having a suitable companion for her, you know, one to replace the rather outmoded, moth eaten, top heavy, lumbering #6604. Patrons even enjoy getting bills now, since they are delivered by our latest addition to the family. I want to thank you very much for the part you played in this blessed event. (Photograph courtesy of the United States Postal Service)

Chevrolet furnished 1,000 three-quarter-ton Model 3442s to the Post Office Department in 1956, plus 1,978 in 1957 and another 1,250 in 1958. These were all standard left-hand-drive vans. The Model 3442 pictured was acquired in 1958.

Chevrolet provided a single right-hand drive three-quarter-ton Model 3602 van to the Post Office Department in 1956 for $3,119.79. The following year, 420 more were furnished at $2,291.92 each. In 1958, an additional 1,875 vans were acquired. These had a price tag of $2,158.30 each. The Model 3602 was the "right-hand" rival to Chevrolet's left-hand drive Model 3442.

A large fleet of Ford Courier station wagons was acquired for Special Delivery service in 1958. The Fords in this photograph were assigned to Washington, D.C. Prior to this, many letter carriers furnished their own vehicles and were reimbursed for mileage or paid an hourly "lease / hire" fee. Postal officials realized that it was cheaper to buy inexpensive vehicles such as these. Despite the smiles in this photograph, the acquisition of these vehicles was frowned upon by the majority of those assigned to drive them. Postal workers considered their automobile allowances to be an important part of their overall pay. They hated the loss of this extra income. By 1967, the Post Office Department still had 12,000 carriers driving their own cars. These carriers were paid an average of $1.15 per hour extra for using their automobiles. A government-sponsored study concluded that about 10 percent of these privately owned vehicles were foreign makes. That study prompted the House Appropriations Committee to eliminate all funding to carriers with foreign automobiles. (Photograph courtesy of George Shifflet)

Only 63 two-and-one-half-ton International Harvester AM-162s were purchased in 1959. These 154-hp trucks were assigned serial numbers 950001 through 950063. Weighing in at 7,750 pounds each, the price tag was $3,898.29 per truck. (Photograph courtesy of Joseph H. Cohen, United States Postal Service, New York City)

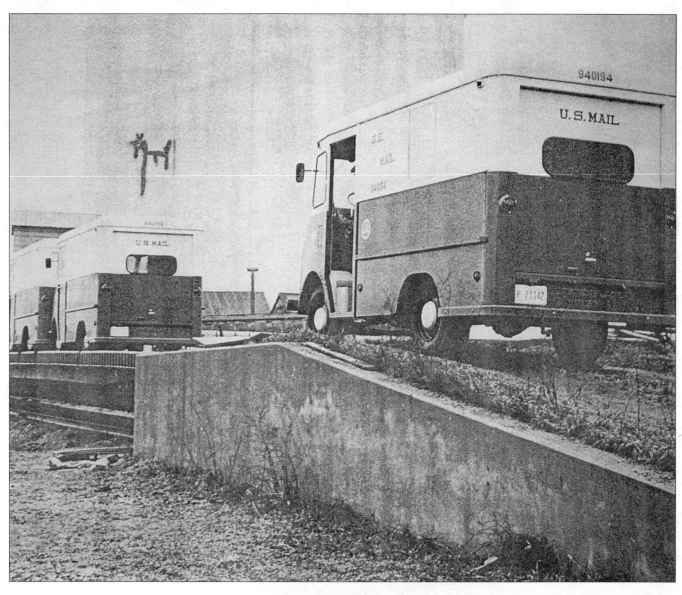

In 1959, the Post Office Department placed an order for 1,500 Dodge M6-P300s. This requisition was worth more than $3.3 million. These three-quarter-ton right-hand drive vans, powered by 120-hp engines, were delivered on flatbed railway cars. According to postal officials, this method of delivery was faster, cheaper and much less dangerous to employees than other forms of delivery.

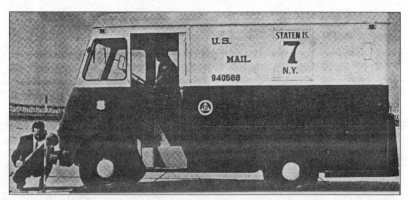

Twenty-nine International Harvester AM-80 "Metro-mites" were purchased in 1959 as a test. These three-quarter-ton right-hand drive vans were judged to be highly maneuverable and particularly economical to operate. Drivers also appreciated the way the vehicle's front-end design furnished an excellent view of tots that might be playing in the street. An additional order of 20 AM-80s was placed in 1960.

One of the 1,200 International Harvester three-quarter-ton Model AM-122 purchased in 1960. These $2,135 trucks were powered by a 112-hp engine. (Photograph courtesy of the Library of Congress)

For more than four decades, from the early 1950s to the present, vans have been the main mules for transporting the mail. Postal vans have come in a wide variety of sizes, from half-ton to two tons, and from a wide assortment of makers. Among the earliest of the half-ton size was a right-hand drive vehicle developed by Willys and Highway Products of Kent, Ohio. These were designated as the Model FDJ-3A "Fleetvans." A 1960 trial model (top) and a full-scale production version (bottom) are pictured. Over 3,200 FDJ-3As were purchased by the postal service in 1960, followed by another order for 800 in 1961. Each of these 1960-1961 "Fleetvans" had a $1,925.53 price tag. What made the purchase of these half-tons so memorable to postal officials in retrospect was not the size of the order, but the number of recalls and modifications that were required to simply keep them roadworthy.

Bearing its "051250" serial number (top), was of the last in a batch of 1,250 two-and-one-half-ton Chevrolet C6302 mail vans delivered to the Post Office Department in 1960. This was a big order, as the bottom view shows. Prior to this shipment, most postal trucks of that size were furnished by International Harvester, which produced 251 in 1958 and 63 in 1959. (Bottom photograph courtesy of the United States Postal Service)

The introduction of the nationwide five-digit ZIP Code scheme in 1963 prompted Studebaker to dub its new 1963 right-hand drive Model 8E5 mini-postal vehicle the "ZIP-Van."

This five-ton 1963 International "Metro" AMC-162 container van never really fit all the roles it was expected to play, despite the fact that it featured a short turning radius, adjustable suspension, and a totally flat cargo area that was ideal for transporting wheeled containers. It was fine as an in-city vehicle, but it didn't survive well on the open road. Its lack of a two-speed differential, its factory installed governor, and its lack of power steering all made it less than ideal over long distances or country roads. At high speeds the rear end was no match for its governed engine, causing excessive revolutions per minute to be a constant problem. Frustrated postal mechanics typically disconnected the governors, replaced the rear ends, and installed power steering units, although none of these retrofits were totally successful.

"Sit and Stand" delivery vehicles, such as this right-hand drive 1965 Jeep, were extremely popular with the Post Office Department. The "Sit/Stand" designation, first used in the 1950s, came from the fact that the driver could operate the vehicle either from a seated or standing position. Typically the driver would stand on short runs and sit down on longer hauls.

Since 1960 vans have always been purchased in big numbers. In 1969, the postal service ordered 6,961 half-ton steel-bodied M-800Ps fabricated using International Harvester components. This represented the bulk of all postal vans purchased that year.

International Harvester received a $14.7 million contract from the government in 1967 for 6,745 "Scouts." These were equipped with the typical four-cylinder, 93-hp engines. They also featured standard hinged doors. These were purchased as replacements for mailsters and postal jeeps. The version depicted here was different from those purchased in 1967 in that it featured sliding side doors and more truck-like front and side mirror assemblies.

The postal version of the Scout was spartan. A heater was the driver's only creature comfort. Among its few mechanical options was an automatic transmission that was shifted from the dash.

Plans to upgrade the Postal Service's fleet began to develop in 1982, when postal officials approved the concept of creating a new "Long-Life Mail Van." In 1983, the Postal Service authorized a competitive testing program for interested manufacturers. Unlike previous contests, this competition was not based upon price. It was a performance-based competition. The winner-take-all contest pitted Grumman Allied Industries with General Motors Truck and Bus Division; Poveco, a joint venture of Fruehauf and General Automotive Corp.; and Ling Temcon Vought/American General Division. This particular vehicle, serial number "0000000," is the Grumman prototype. The Postal Service's procurement plan called for the expenditure of about $1 billion to acquire the new-style vehicle. The showdown between the three vehicles took place at the Uniroyal Test Facility at Laredo, Texas, in 1985. Of the three test vehicles, only the Grumman/General Motors product survived testing. The Grumman Allied Industries vehicle is built on the frame and powertrain of a General Motors modified S10 chassis. The four-cylinder inline gasoline-type engine and three-speed automatic transmission have a projected life expectancy of 12 years. The new right-hand drive mail vans are equipped with power steering and have a curb weight of 3,008 pounds. The body of the vehicle, made by Grumman, is of corrosion-resistant aluminum and is designed to have a life expectancy of 24 years, three times the planned life of any vehicle currently in the Postal Service fleet.

In recent years the Postal Service has stopped using brand names on its vehicles. It has been removing the manufacturers' nameplates and trademarks from most of its older vehicles and has demanded that new vehicles come without the manufacturer's identification whenever possible. Among the first of the vehicles affected by the brand name ban were Volvo/White/GMC Class 7 cargo vans. One hundred-and-eighty-nine Model FE42 seventon vans were purchased in 1991 at a cost of $41,517 each, along with 184 nine-ton versions. The cost of the nine-ton FE42s was $41,817 each. (Photograph courtesy of Paul Rosenak)

Jeeps proved their reliability during World War II. On countless battlefields around the world they repeatedly demonstrated just how rugged and reliable they were. Many GIs swore by them, believing they could go just about anywhere and do nearly anything. In some respects, servicemen imbued them with flesh and blood-like qualities. Postal workers also had a long-term love affair with the Willys Jeep and American Motors General Corp. DJ-5 "Dispatcher," one that began almost from the moment it was created in the late 1960s until production ceased in the 1980s. During that span more than 130,000 were built, making it the longest continuing single model vehicle made. It should be noted that while to many Americans all postal jeeps probably look alike, over the years the Postal Service has actually used at least nine distinct types of DJ-5s. The DJ-5E (Electrics) and the DJ-5G (1978s with alternative engines) were considered unique to the postal jeep family. These particular postal jeeps did not survive the flooding in the area of Johnstown, Pennsylvania, in 1977.

Postal vans, such as this one in New York City, have been used for decades to transport letter carriers to their routes.

Street scene outside a New York City postal facility in the 1950s. Among the parked postal vehicles is a two-ton Dodge B-3-G along the right curb. Several three-quarter ton International 122s are on the left side of the street.

127

Mail being loaded aboard the first helicopter used to transport mail from the 30th Street Heliport in New York City. The vehicle is a 1956 three-quarter ton International SM-122.

Trucks from five New York City postal stations in 1961 making direct connections with a transcontinental plane to help ensure next-day delivery of California mail. (Photograph courtesy of the United States Postal Service)

Driver training was provided by the postal service to operators of all new vehicles, including these mailsters photographed in 1961. (Photograph courtesy of the United States Postal Service)

The research department of the postal service helped to design seat belts for the operators of "Sit / Stand" vehicles in 1963. This particular type of restraint included an inertia reel for normal movement by the driver but that locked under sudden impact. (Photograph courtesy of the United States Postal Service)

Five-ton International Harvester truck, photographed new in 1964. This 750 cubic-foot capacity truck featured a flat floor and air bag suspension. (Photograph courtesy of the United States Postal Service)

"Igloo" containers of mail being loaded for night shipment in 1968 by a Boeing 727 "Quick-Change" jet. (Photograph courtesy of the United States Postal Service)

The Post Office Department performed an array of safety tests on its vehicles in 1968 to determine performance standards. (Photograph courtesy of the United States Postal Service)

This GMC mail truck is used at Washington National Airport. The large "7" on the side enables air-traffic controllers and airport managers to easily identify mail trucks on the field.

Early morning before service begins.

Notice the difference? This pair of 1986 two-ton GMC mail trucks at Washington, D.C., feature different reflective striping. The one on the right shows the current style, while the vehicle on the left is awaiting a new paint job and the re-application of its new red, white and blue striping.

A new one-ton 1996 GMC Utilmaster for use in making parcel deliveries

Currently, the United States Postal Service operates a $5.5 billion transportation network. (Photograph courtesy of the United States Postal Service)

This 1954 Ford Courier was used in New York City for making special deliveries. (Photograph courtesy of Joseph Cohn, United States Postal Service, New York City)

RURAL DELIVERY VEHICLES

USA

2

Chapter **2**

This automobile, manufactured by the Church Manufacturing Co., holds the distinction of being the earliest known motor vehicle used in rural mail service. The machine was tested on a route out of Adrian, Michigan, from November 28, 1902, to January 3, 1903. The test was successful enough to show that it was only a matter of time before automobiles became commonplace on rural routes. (The vehicle did not complete the route on two of the trail days because of deep snowdrifts and partially frozen mud.) Only about 2-1/2 gallons of gasoline were consumed on each trip at a cost of 15 cents per gallon. This was considered substantially less than the cost of horse feed. The motor vehicle completed the route in about half the time normally required by a horse-drawn mail wagon. The experiment was paid for by the Bond Steel Post Co., makers of the particular mailboxes used along the Adrian mail route. (Photograph courtesy of the National Rural Letters Association)

This Model A "Orient Buckboard," produced by the Waltham Manufacturing Co., was used in 1904 by rural letter carrier W.A. Dingley on his route at Pratts Junction, Massachusetts. The owner confessed that "When I bought the machine (which was manufactured at Waltham, Massachusetts) I knew no more about a gasoline engine than I now know about the dead languages, and the first time I ran it over my (24 mile) route I inadvertently stopped the engine 14 times by attempting to start the machine with the brake set or with the spark retarded ... however, it was not long before I could cover the whole route without stopping the engine."

While most motorized rural letter carriers used their vehicles only in good weather, North Baltimore, Ohio, carrier Jay Radebaugh used his seven-hp Oldsmobile runabout all the time. In all kinds of weather, winter or summer, rain or shine, he relied on his Oldsmobile. In the summer Radebaugh departed from the post office at 9:15 a.m., served 178 mailboxes, delivered or collected from 6,000 to 8,000 pieces of mail per month, and was back by 2 p.m. In the winter he also left at 9:15 a.m. but returned to the post office by 4 p.m.

The seven-hp, Type E Rambler was purchased by D.W. Edie for use on his 25-mile route, which originated from Hall's Corners, New York. The automobile enabled Edie to complete his route in about three hours, far faster than when he delivered mail by horse-drawn mail wagon. He used some of the time that he saved to rent his vehicle for delivery purposes.

James T. Mullikin purchased this 10-hp Cadillac for use on his mail route out of Trappe, Maryland. He figured that the purchase was actually a great deal. The two horses he owned previously ate $25 per month, while the price of gasoline at $5.20 a month made a difference of $19.80 in favor of the Cadillac. Mullikin also was able to complete his 27-mile mail route two hours faster in the car than by horse. This enabled him to use the machine to transport paying passengers from place to place when he was not on duty. In many cases this added about $7 a day to his salary.

The Post Office Department tested the feasibility of using motorized vehicles for rural free delivery, using a pair of four-hp Waltham Manufacturing Co. "Orient Buckboards" outside Washington, D.C., in the summer of 1906. Weighing about 650 pounds each, these vehicles were powered by a single-cylinder, air-cooled, gasoline engine. During the month-long trials, from June 2 to July 3, the two test vehicles were found to cut routine delivery times over the 24-mile routes by about half. The cost of operating each vehicle was about four cents per mile, far less than a comparable horse-drawn route, and neither experienced any significant mechanical difficulty. The average speed was about four miles per hour. The routes included 58 sharp turns, grades of up to 40 degrees, and a great number of ditches, gullies, ruts and rocks. Postal officials specifically picked the routes around Washington so that they could closely monitor the tests. They concluded that "The adaptability of motor transportation to rural service having thus received favorable demonstration, the question of its practicability as applied to all sections of the country remains a matter of consideration."

Priced at $475, the 1908 Pietsch Auto Co. "Paco" runabout with a special R.F.D. body was described as "the only practical machine for the service of the R.F.D. Boys." Another alternative was this Paco delivery wagon, which was $25 more. Both the runabout and the wagon were powered by a two-cylinder, four-cycle engine that was capable of delivering up to 20 hp.

Offered in 1908, this King Motor Vehicle Co. Model A motor wagon was said to be "The most practical motor wagon in the world for mail carriers." It was powered by a two-cylinder, dual chain-drive, air-cooled engine that produced 12 hp. Priced at $490, the terms of sale were one-half when ordered and the remainder "Collect-on-Delivery."

George Howe used this home-styled mail truck for his route in Oregon. (Photograph courtesy of the United States Postal Service)

This Brush runabout was used by M.A. Detwiler, a rural letter carrier assigned to the Three Springs, Pennsylvania, post office in 1910. (Photograph courtesy of the National Rural Carriers Association)

One of the earliest mail routes established in the United States provided service to residents around Climax, Michigan. This route was started on December 3, 1896. The first mailbox on this route belonged to H.H. Pierce. To commemorate the 14th anniversary of service in 1910, Climax's postmaster, Morris Arnold, joined letter carrier Louis Clark in delivering the mail to Pierce's mailbox. Standing in front of the mailbox is Pierce's granddaughter, Bethel Pierce Ebinger.

Model T Ford roadsters were popular among rural letter carriers. They could be used "as is" or easily adapted to postal use by simply replacing the deck-mounted rumbleseat with a commercial or homemade box body.

A whopping price tag of about $1,000 and a hefty weight of approximately 2,000 pounds when fully fitted made this 1912 one-half ton International Harvester "Auto Wagon" with its special "RFD body" less than an appealing purchase. Few rural carriers even bothered to inquire about this vehicle when advertisements for it first appeared early in the summer of 1912. By summer's end, the ad campaign was abruptly stopped because of poor sales. Despite its limited appeal, the vehicle had some novel features. The body had five cabinets, each provided with pigeonholes and a large receptacle for newspapers and periodicals. Smaller compartments were provided in the cab for storing postage stamps, postal cards, stamped envelopes, and other salable government products. Each drawer and cabinet was dustproof, water tight, and lockable; and the body could be removed in a matter of minutes, transforming this mail vehicle into a light delivery wagon. Power was provided by a two-cylinder (horizontally opposed), air-cooled, 18-hp engine. Dual acetone head lamps and a pair of cowl lamps were among the available options.

Designated by International as Model MA, this 1913 half-ton version featured an exceptionally uncommon enclosed auto-bus-like body. In addition to its high wheels, which were typical of International Harvester vehicles until 1915, a feature that was favored for operating under muddy or snowy conditions, the rear wheels of this mail vehicle were fitted with snow chains. (Photograph courtesy of the United States Postal Service)

Rural carrier J.W. Morton was 70 years old when this photograph was taken. By then, he had been serving on the same Collinsville, Ohio, route since October 15, 1896. This was one of the first rural mail routes established in Ohio. It also was one of the earliest to be served by automobile. Morton started using a motor vehicle in 1911. Recounting his 19 years of service in 1915, Morton stated that "Very few days have been missed. Occasionally I have to miss a few days on account of the roads being blocked with snow."

In 1915, the Post Office Department received 2,422 petitions for new RFD routes. Of those, 1,257 routes were given serious consideration and 721 were established. Many of these were motorized routes. Standish, Michigan, had three motorized routes in 1915. These varied from 23 to 28 miles in length. On average, Standish's rural carriers delivered approximately 40,000 pieces of mail each month.

Leaving from Shelby, Michigan, in 1915 in his six month old Ford, rural carrier H.G. Kage usually transported about 300 pounds of mail per trip. Kage was exceptionally pleased with the performance of his Ford, boasting that it had withstood its first Michigan winter without a breakdown or a punctured tire.

Florida rural carrier Frank Green was proud to use his new 1915 Saxon "delivery car" on his 14-mile mail route. Except for the 49-inch high by 37-inch long delivery body that could accommodate a 400-pound load, this four-cylinder Saxon was identical to the company's roadster — and the similarities included matching price tags of $395. In this particular case, the load amounted to 549 pieces of mail weighing 127 pounds. Saxon's delivery car model included storm curtains at the side for use in bad weather.

International Harvester offered a special mail-oriented version of its 1915 Model MA, one that specifically complied with government mail truck specifications. These requirements were not hard to comply with. Among other things, they called for a full top, storm curtains, and a screened body. This particular vehicle provided a half-ton capacity within its 90 cubic foot body. Its high artillery spoke wheels were expected to be a major selling point, especially among rural carriers who preferred this style of wheel. The engine was a horizontally-opposed two-cylinder, air-cooled unit that furnished about 19 hp. Excluding shipping charges from International's Akron, Ohio, factory, the base price of this rural mail truck was $655.

Only halfway done and he still had plenty of mail yet to deliver, Gramplan, Pennsylvania, rural letter carrier Edwin Spencer stopped at his house for lunch the day that this photograph was taken (September 7, 1916). Spencer, who began working for the postal service in 1900, had the luxury of living along his route. This enabled him to check in with the family at least once during the day.

An old wagon wheel, such as this one outside of Middleport, Ohio, made the ideal "Lazy Susan" for rural mailboxes. Such wheels enabled carriers to fill many mailboxes without moving.

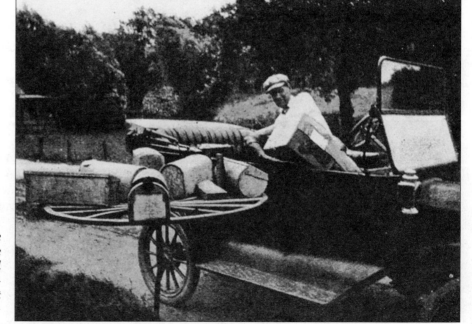

Half-ton Willys right-hand drive FDJ-3A purchased in 1961. (Photo courtesy of the United States Postal Service)

Boasting chrome wheels and other accents, this Ford Bronco, used by the Postal Service Police in Washington, D.C., is a high-class protection service vehicle.

Otherwise invisible amidst snow, the red, white and blue reflective strips and the Postal Service logo make trucks more visible.

In 1995, the Postal Service deployed six "ELLVs" (Electric Long-Life Vehicles) to six locations selected because they afforded a wide range of temperature extremes and driving conditions. This particular vehicle, utilizing an advanced lead acid battery, was assigned to Merrifield, Virginia. (Photo courtesy of the United States Postal Service)

President Franklin Delano Roosevelt mailed the first official letter inaugurating highway mail service from this bus in 1941. Forty-five years later, this historic postal vehicle required a complete restoration. The interior was systematically emptied and the flooring carefully removed. All the old glass, much of it broken long ago, was taken out and the entire vehicle was hand- and machine-sanded both inside and out. To make this vehicle operative again, the powertrain, brakes, steering, and electrical systems also were totally rebuilt. This restoration was made possible by a grant from the members of the American Postal Workers Union, AFL-CIO. (Photograph by Jeff Tinsley, Smithsonian Institution)

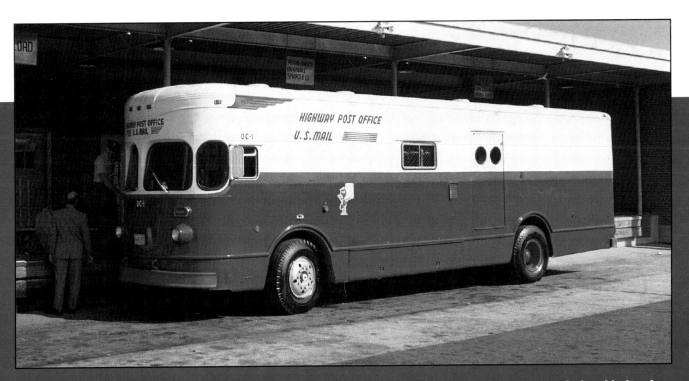

Twin Coach Highway Post Office used in the 1960s. (Photo courtesy of the United States Postal Service)

Between 1960 and 1963 the Post Office Department tested 77 electric vehicles in six locations nationwide. (Photo courtesy of the United States Postal Service)

The postal Jeep, this a 1963 model, was a common site in many residential neighborhoods. (Old Cars photo)

Some local post offices are truly mobile units.
(Photo courtesy of the United States Postal Service)

One of the three competitors in the challenging test to create a new "Long-Life Vehicle" for the United States Postal Service. This model was one of the losers.

Over the years the Postal Service has tried various electric vehicles, including this unsuccessful, yet modernistic looking version.

This fully restored Model A Ford mail truck is on display at the National Postal Museum in Washington, D.C. (Photograph by Jeff Tinsley and Richard Strauss, Smithsonian Institution)

Forward control vans were used largely for mail collections.

This Ford Model T with a "Snowbird Attachment" was used for Rural Free Delivery Service at Central Square, New York. The vehicle was used by letter carrier Harold Crabtree during the 1920s and 1930s.

One of 1,250 three-quarter-ton Chevrolet Model 344s acquired in 1958 for $2,298.90 each. (Photo courtesy of the United States Postal Service)

To promote the purchase of a large number of Hudson/Essex Phaetons in 1920 for Rural Free Delivery, the manufacturer sent four vehicles on a transcontinental odyssey. This Essex was the first to finish the San Francisco to New York run, completing the trip in four days, 14 hours, and 43 minutes.

Rural carrier John Lindsey's first car was a stunning new 1924 Model T Ford roadster. Lindsey was extremely proud of his shiny black roadster, but within a matter of weeks he realized that his new car lacked sufficient space to transport all the mail. He was able to rectify this shortcoming by trading up for this Model T touring car. Back then you could trade up by paying the difference between the two models. In this case the difference was $35. Lindsey began carrying mail in 1920 and retired after 58 years. Years after his retirement he recalled that he used the Model T as much as possible, but the way he figured it, he spent about as much time driving it as he did digging it out of the mud. Lindsey didn't go anywhere without a shovel and an ax. The ax was for chopping down small trees that could be used to pry the tires out of the mud when they got stuck. Lindsey traded cars about every three or four years. His philosophy on how to treat a new car was simple: "You may as well take something and scratch it at the start just to get it over with!"

A hybrid vehicle that was more Model A Ford than anything else, the Eskimobile with its "HiStilt" wheels was ideal for traversing deep snow. (Photograph courtesy of The Nebraska Rural Letter Carrier)

Letter carrier Melvin Young purchased this Ford V-8 in 1936 for use on his Pennsylvania route.

The arrival of the rural carrier was like a magnet at Lake Dick, a 1938 Farm Security Administration project in Phillips County, Arkansas, instantly bringing neighbors together. (Photograph courtesy of the Library of Congress)

Rural carrier Lloyd Mortice developed this unique snowmobile for use on his route in New England. To avoid becoming snowbound, he acquired steel tracks from a supplier and developed skis for the front of his 1926 Model T Ford. The firm that sold Mortice the tank-like treads liked his idea so much that it later produced a similar vehicle for commercial use.

The simple addition of a "Snow-Flyer" package was all that was required to transform a normal Ford into a four-wheel drive, positive belt traction snowmobile. (Photograph courtesy of The Nebraska Rural Letter Carrier)

In the late-1920s, a commercially produced "Snow-bird Attachment" ensured greater winter mobility for rural letter carriers. Different ski configurations existed, including some that fastened onto the front wheel rims, while others replaced the front wheels altogether. In either case, the skis, tank treads and inner pair of rear tires were removable within a matter of minutes for hard-surface driving. Such half-track gear was a fairly common purchase among Model T drivers in areas of the country prone to snow.

Residents near Ledyard, Connecticut, gathered at a crossroads to receive mail on November 19, 1940. This photograph was taken by Jack Delano for the Farm Security Administration. (Photograph courtesy of the Library of Congress)

This Studebaker sedan was used in 1946 in Pennsylvania. Because they typically grew up in the communities they served, rural carriers had a special relationship with their customers. Knowing that the mail often contained bad news, during World War II rural carriers often took government-looking letters to their neighbors after routine hours. That way they could stay to console their friends if the news was especially unpleasant.

From time to time the Post Office Department had considered doing what rural carriers considered to be "the unthinkable" — furnishing government-owned or leased vehicles instead of furnishing an allowance to rural carriers to provide their own vehicles. Rural carriers received their first allowances for equipment maintenance in 1925, when Congress approved a four-cents-per-mile measure. That remained the allowance until 1934 when a one-cent-per-mile increase was authorized. The five cent limit remained in effect until 1946, followed by another one cent increase in 1948. By 1952, the allowance was increased to nine cents per mile, with a minimum of $3 a day for heavy carrier routes. One idea was to provide some sort of standard vehicle, such as this 1953 Willys jeep, instead of allowing the hodgepodge of vehicles used by rural carriers. Because of the costs associated with such a plan, the idea quickly died. This particular model of jeep was a left-hand rural delivery model that featured four-wheel drive for all-year transportation. Like other jeeps at the time, it was powered by a four-cylinder "Hurricane" engine.

Since its introduction in 1991, over 4,600 Subaru right-hand drive versions of its popular "Legacy" station wagon have been produced primarily for rural letter carriers. These are fully-equipped all-wheel drive vehicles. They include a four-speed automatic transmission, power-assisted four-wheel disc brakes, power steering, power windows, 40-watt AM/FM stereo cassette radio, and a full-size spare tire as standard equipment. (Photograph courtesy of Subaru of America)

Despite the absence of right-hand steering, Chevrolet "Blazers" have been popular among rural letter carriers. Major selling points have included their exceptional cargo capacity and ability to drive in foul weather.

This advertisement for the Orient Buckboard appeared in the December 1905 issue of R.F.D. News. *This vehicle was said to be designed especially for rural letter carriers. According to the manufacturer, "carriers have made valuable suggestions and have cooperated with the company in arriving at a practical, dependable and economical machine."*

Sumter, South Carolina, rural letter carrier J.A. Schwerin, Jr., began using this automobile over his 28-mile route in July 1905. His view was that "I would not think of driving an old plug again and a rattle-trap buggy."

The mud on this Oldsmobile, photographed in 1905, appears to weigh about as much as the vehicle itself.

A.H. Helgeson of Montevideo, Minnesota, purchased this Oldsmobile in July 1904 for use on his 25-mile route. Helgeson was pleased with his runabout, boasting that "I had one breakdown, so that I had to borrow a horse to pull me and the machine home."

Oldsmobile

PRICE, $650

The prime requisite in an automobile for rural delivery work is satisfactory service.

SATISFACTORY SERVICE MEANS :

First—Reasonable cost of maintenance. Second—Freedom from any tendency to get out of order. Third—Durability to stand the wear and tear of use. Fourth—Power to climb hills and take you along as fast as you want to go. Fifth—Must be easy to start and easy to stop—always under perfect control. Sixth—It must be dependable in emergencies.

The latest type of Oldsmobile Standard Runabout meets these requirements more fully than any other car. Note a few of the distinctive features of this car:

Its new type of side springs makes it wonderfully easy riding, and are a revelation in improved spring suspension. The ratchet brake, which acts on a drum attached directly to the front sprocket, has been substituted for the deferential brake. External hub brakes are used which relieve themselves under all conditions. In starting, the spark is retarded automatically, so that all danger of back fire is removed. Lamp and horn equipment is furnished with these cars. We will gladly arrange for a demonstration of this or any of our cars at your convenience.

It will pay YOU to consider the Oldsmobile Runabout for use on your R. F. D. route. Write us for particulars. Address Dept. RD.

OLDS MOTOR WORKS
Detroit, U. S. A.
Member A. L. A. M.

Oldsmobile advertisement published in a 1905 issue of R.F.D. News.

V.E. Barnett of Colfax, Indiana, acquired this Oldsmobile in March 1905 for use on his 27-mile mail route.

South Dakota rural letter carrier C.G. Moffitt, photographed in 1904 with his Oldsmobile eight-horsepower runabout purchased on January 15, 1904. Writing in R.F.D. News in August 1905, Moffitt noted that "Last year I ran the auto until December 20, and then laid it up only because I had no windshield in front as it was too cold for my face." Moffitt estimated that he could complete his 32-mile route in about half the time using this automobile, as compared to his horse-drawn wagon.

This Oldsmobile was used between November 28, 1902, and January 3, 1903, to serve rural patrons outside of Adrian, Michigan.

The Orient Buckboard was powered by a single-cylinder four-horsepower engine. The engine transferred power through two friction discs, shown here in detail. The disc on the engine shaft had a metal face and the wheel that engaged it was covered with a special fibroid material that had a high degree of adhesion. The driving mechanism turned a shaft, which was attached by twin chains to the rear wheels.

CONTRACTOR VEHICLES

USA
3

Chapter 3

A contract "stage line" was operated in 1906 between Roswell and Torrance, New Mexico, by the Roswell Automobile Co. using two Winton Motor Carriage Co. runabouts. The distance between those two points was 101 miles. Actually, each car covered only half that distance. Passengers and mail were exchanged at a "halfway house." At this midway point a mechanic was onhand to make any necessary repairs. Occasionally during each of the four-hour jaunts, passengers would be allowed to stop to shoot antelope. The Post Office Department paid $42 a day for this daily service. That amount was augmented by passenger fares, which usually amounted to an additional $30 a day. This particular mail route was highly profitable. Average monthly receipts amounted to about $2,000. Expenses — including paying the drivers $75 a month, the mechanic $100 a month, and a cook $60 a month for preparing meals at the halfway house, plus tires and gasoline — reportedly amounted to only about $800.

Star Route contractors transported mail between cities. Often such routes were hundreds of miles. The name "Star Route" was derived from a shortcut used in recording such postal contracts. Prior to 1845, the practice of the Post Office Department was to award mail contracts to the lowest bidder tendering sufficient guaranty for faithful performance, without any reference to the mode of transportation that may be necessary to provide for "celerity (swiftness), certainty, and security." In keeping with this, these bids were classified as "celerity, certainty and security" bids. Presumably to avoid the constant need for writing out those three words over and over again in the record books of the Post Office Department, the clerks in the Contracts Division designated them in the Postal Route Registers by placing three stars before their listing. Subsequently, because of this form of shorthand they became know as "star bids." In past decades, these contractors also frequently operated bus lines over these same mail routes. Hours after this photograph was taken in front of the post office at Smullton, Pennsylvania, this 1912 International Harvester bus was all but destroyed. The bus served the Star Route between Rebersburg and Coburn, a distance of about eight miles. Upon its return run it toppled down an embankment about two miles west of Smullton. The driver was thrown from the vehicle almost immediately and suffered only slight bruises. The lone passenger was trapped inside the wreckage as it rolled downhill, but he, too, escaped with only minor injuries.

The truck stage between Manchester and Londonderry, Vermont, also transported mail under contract to the Post Office Department.

To prove the feasibility of long distance Parcel Post Service a contractor-operated Autocar screen-side truck was run between Lancaster, Pennsylvania, and New York City on March 20, 1918. The 180-mile trip took 10 hours. The truck was loaded with 1,920 pounds of mail, none of which was letters. The shipment consisted of eggs, butter, honey and day-old chicks. This experiment proved to postal officials that farmers within a 180-mile radius of New York City could easily supply food by mail to the city's residents. A few months before this trial the Post Office Department launched a "Farm-to-Table" program that was designed to link willing farmers with urban consumers anxious to purchase farm-fresh products without having to deal with a middleman. This experiment in consumerism was a modest success.

This GMC passenger van was used in 1918 to transport both mail and travelers over a Star Route.

Star Route contractors, such as this one from Liberal, Kansas, had to be careful about transporting liquor between "wet" and "dry" states. While postal service regulations prohibited Star Route contractors from hauling alcoholic beverages, drivers never knew what actually was in the mailbags they were transporting.

Many highway motor coach companies, such as the Pioneer Stage Lines, realized that mail contracts were a profitable sideline. In this case, under a 1930s contract with the Post Office Department, Pioneer transported mail sacks along with its paying passengers, between Salmon, Challis and MacKay, Idaho. Actually, two postal contracts applied to this 116-mile route. One was between Salmon to Challis, a distance of 62 miles, while the other was from Challis and MacKay, 54 miles apart. These were designated as Star Route numbers 70154 and 70194, respectively. Under the terms of its contracts with the Post Office Department, service was to be furnished six days a week. Speed was always an issue. In good weather the postal service expected the Challis and MacKay run to be completed in 154 minutes, while the Challis and Salmon route could take as many as 180 minutes. In bad weather postal officials were more lenient, upping the time to 24 hours. Besides whatever passengers and baggage there might be, the contractor was required to transport up to 2,000 pounds of mail if the need arose. Obviously these two Pioneer contracts were profitable, so much so that the

There were some Star Routes that no one wanted. Because the route between Price and Vernal, Utah, was so long and the terrain was so bad, it had to be operated by Uncle Sam beginning shortly before World War I. The route included snow packed roads at 1,800 foot elevations, to desert-like conditions. Much of the time the mail trucks operated in convoys that were pulled in tandem by a powerful tractor. During the first year of operation the government's mail trucks hauled about 700,000 pounds of mail each month.

With the introduction of Parcel Post, many contract mail routes were deluged with parcels, so much so that contractors no longer wanted to bid on them. This was made worse by the fact that some routes were just too hard to operate under normal circumstances, let alone when there was a mound of mail that had to be moved. One of the worst routes was between Price and Vernal, Utah, a 125-mile route. In the winter months Utah snows in this region could reach depths of eight feet or more. Under the circumstances contractors declined bidding on this particular route, forcing the government to operate it. In 1919, six routes were operated by the government, including the one between Price and Vernal. Government reports put a good face on the fact that no one else wanted these routes, with statements such as "The establishment of these routes has demonstrated that it is not only a more economical service (which it wasn't), but that schedules can be more closely maintained (which wasn't the case either), and the mail in greater volume can be more carefully and expeditiously handled (another untruth)." Such glowing, yet untrue, announcements were accompanied with other sugar-coated statements such as "This [better service] is due to the better equipment, properly maintained, which is used, and to the further fact that more efficient men are employed by the department than by private contractors, who naturally endeavor to provide the service required at the lowest possible cost." While the government's employees may not have actually been more efficient than those that might have been furnished by a contractor, they certainly proved themselves to be creative. To keep the mail moving, the government used this Caterpillar tractor to pull convoys of mail trucks into the Uintah Basin.

The Price to Vernal route continued to be a white elephant. In 1925, the Post Office Department again issued a request for bids among private contractors willing to take on this service, noting that this route was "not now under contract" but that it was "operated with departmental equipment." Again, no outside contractor took up the government on this offer either.

Not known for its stylish appointments, nevertheless Studebaker's "Light-Six" Model EM touring car was respected for its performance and durability. This stripped down version was certainly pushed to the limit. Studebaker claimed that its all steel body touring car could comfortably accommodate five passengers. This one clearly could, if the fifth space wasn't taken up by mail sacks. Priced at $1,485, this 2,650-pound car featured a six-cylinder inline engine that provided about 40 hp. Oversized headlamps and fuel efficiency were among its most noteworthy features. It was not uncommon for Model EMs to achieve 18 to 22 miles per gallon under normal loads and driving conditions.

173

This GMC tractor, with trailer, was used in the 1950s on the Houston to San Antonio "T-Route." T-Routes were not much different from "Star Routes" (routes over which mail was transported by private contractors working for the postal service). The difference was that while any type of vehicle might be used on a Star Route, only a truck could be used on T-Route. (Photograph courtesy of the United States Postal Service)

These two 1949 International Harvester KB-7s, photographed at the loading dock of the Hagerstown, Maryland, post office, along with a Dodge panel truck and a three-ton Dodge tractor with trailer, were used by short-haul mail contractors. (Photograph courtesy of Stuart Abraham)

Ralph Rohrer held the mail contract between Hagerstown, Maryland, and Harrisburg, Pennsylvania, in the early 1950s. He used this 1951 International Harvester L-160 over that "T-Route." These were truck routes that operated between specific cities. (Photograph courtesy of Stuart Abraham)

This International Harvester KB-8 tractor transported mail under contract with the Post Office Department in Maryland in 1951. The trailer body, which was built by Thompson Trailer Co., used "sandwiched" aluminum panels to enclose a honeycomb core. This unusual type of construction provided a great deal of wall strength, without the need for roof bows and supporting posts. (Photograph by Frank Alexander)

Big rigs aren't the only way contractors move the mail. This Alaskan Star Route contractor uses a motorized snowsled to transport mail. (Photograph courtesy of the United States Postal Service)

Many contemporary Star Route trucks, such as the two tractor-trailer rigs belonging to Pals Cartage of South Holland, Illinois, (top) and the rig belonging to Dale Foreman of Detroit, Michigan, (bottom) are largely indistinguishable from any other typical truck on the highway. (Photographs courtesy of the National Star Route Contractors Association)

In an attempt to increase the Postal Service's presence on the highways, Star Route contractors such as R.B. Matheson of Douglas City, California (top), and Alan Ritchey of Valley View, Texas (bottom), have been encouraged to make the fact that they are mail contractors as visible as possible. (Photographs courtesy of the National Star Route Contractors Association)

Photograph of the first trip of the Seattle-to-Anchorage highway mail service contract in 1962. (Photograph courtesy of the United States Postal Service)

The first direct shipment of containerized mail to Europe consisted of a truckload of National Geographic magazines sent from Chicago to London in 1965. (Photograph courtesy of the United States Postal Service)

A containerized shipment of bulk mail being loaded onto a trailer for piggyback mail movement in 1968. (Photograph courtesy of the United States Postal Service)

ARMORED
VEHICLES

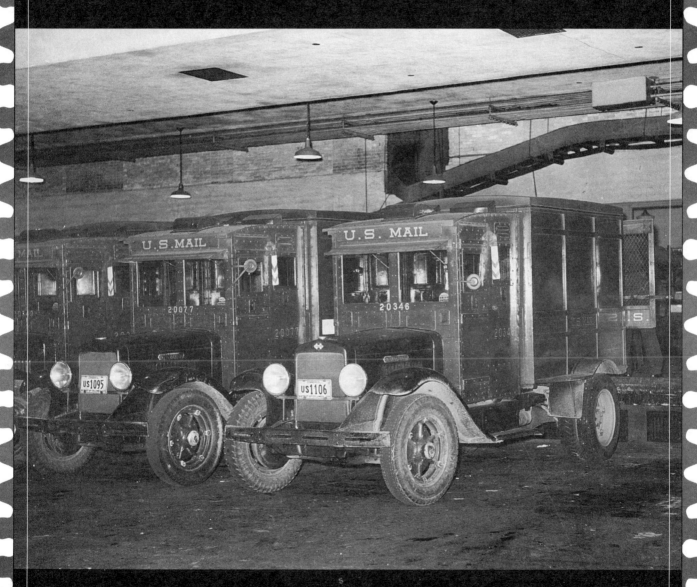

USA

Chapter *4*

A rash of mail truck robberies in the early 1920s prompted the Post Office Department to purchase its first armored trucks. To show how invulnerable these trucks were to gunfire — and to hopefully deter further robberies — photographs such as this, taken in December 1921 outside Washington, D.C., were widely circulated to national newspapers.

The need for additional armored trucks grew in the 1920s. This photograph, taken on November 9, 1925, at the rear of Post Office Department headquarters in Washington, D.C., shows Postmaster General Harry New standing beside one of the new bandit-proof mail trucks. The cab was crafted by the Baldwin Locomotive Works. Seated inside the cab, with gun in-hand, is First Assistant Postmaster General John H. Bartlett. (Photograph courtesy of the Library of Congress)

By the late 1920s, the number of mail truck robberies had dropped significantly. This left postal officials with a false sense of security. By 1930, mail robberies were once again on the increase, prompting the Post Office Department to acquire an additional 280 armored mail trucks, such as this White Motor Co. truck. The screen-bodies for these trucks were purchased separately. This particular truck was assigned to the Washington, D.C., post office. The government decided not to buy many more large armored vehicles, figuring that the growing postal fleet was a sufficient enough deterrent. It was reasoned that by the 1940s, there were so many large postal trucks that a potential robber was unlikely to know precisely which truck held valuable mail. (Photograph courtesy of the United States Postal Service)

In the 1930s, Autocar furnished many of the heavy-duty armored trucks, including this one that was used in Washington, D.C. (Photograph courtesy of the United States Postal Service)

The Post Office Department acquired over 1,800 bulletproof cabs over a three-year period from 1931 to 1933, principally for use in major cities with a Federal Reserve Bank. These were mounted on heavy-duty International Harvester A3-1/2 chassis. The cabs, built by the famed Baldwin Locomotive Works, were equipped with bulletproof glass and gun ports that gave a clear field of fire in every direction. (Photograph courtesy of the United States Postal Service)

Interior view of an armored Baldwin cab mounted on top of an International A3-1/2 chassis.

The postal service classified this 1935 three-quarter-ton International C-1 delivery truck as a light armored car. The truck also featured branded Firestone tires. Although barely visible, the "U.S. Mail" brand was applied to reduce the likelihood of internal theft.

HIGHWAY POST OFFICES

HIGHWAY POST OFFICE
U. S. MAIL

USA
Chapter 5

As part of its 1920 holiday "Mail Early" campaign, the Washington, D.C., post office fitted one of its larger trucks to act as a roving post office. This special mobile "XMAS Post Office," complete with a costumed Santa Claus, made its debut on November 30, 1920.

This Moreland Motor Truck Co. Model S-D "Fast Freight" chassis, with a specially constructed body that would enable a crew of postal workers to perform what was essentially Railway Mail Service on a Star Route, was proposed in 1928. When mail service by rail was discontinued between Tacoma and Morton, Washington, Moreland stepped forward with an offer to provide the vehicle and the service associated with a highway mail route for $12,000. The Post Office Department declined the offer.

In 1928, W.B. Fageol, vice-president of Twin Coach Co. of Kent, Ohio, proposed selling this style of bus to the Post Office Department as a "miniature highway mail car." The postal service declined this unsolicited offer saying that there was no need for mail distribution using any sort of highway vehicle. That view would change within two decades.

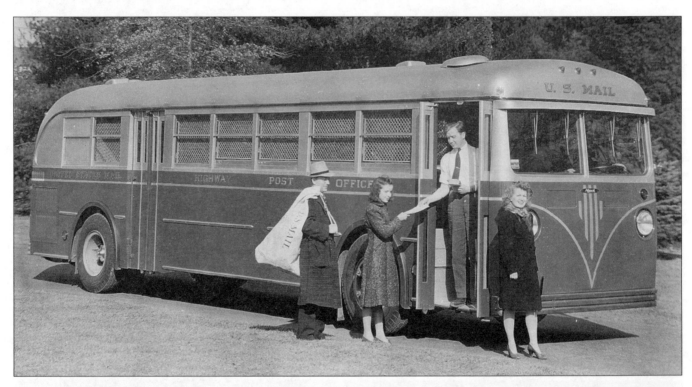

The second of three experimental Highway Post Office routes established in 1941 was inaugurated between South Bend, Peru, and Indianapolis, Indiana — a round trip distance of 302 miles. A different type of vehicle was tested on each route. The three types included a White Motor Co. bus with a "pancake" engine, a modified International Harvester tractor-trailer, and this "pusher-type" Mack bus with its engine in the rear. The Mack was delivered to the Post Office Department on April 21, 1941. The cost of the 33-foot-long Mack was $11,625 (F.O.B. Allentown, Pennsylvania). The weight of this Model CM SPECIAL bus was approximately 18,500 pounds. This vehicle did not prove to be completely practical. The capacity of its gasoline tank was its biggest limitation. Its 80-gallon tank was not sufficient to cover an entire round trip. Operating at 3-1/2 miles per gallon, it was always necessary to refuel at some intermediate point. Because of this, only a small number of Mack buses subsequently entered service.

This adaptation of a Model 788 White transit bus was the nation's first Highway Post Office. It was built of Duraluminum, an alloy that was noted for lightness and strength. The vehicle measured 33 feet from bumper to bumper. In passenger service, such a bus could accommodate up to 40 passengers. As a Highway Post Office, it carried a three-man crew, including the driver. This bus was well equipped for handling mail. Near the front of the bus was a sorting table, with extensive pigeonholes located immediately above. Strong steel racks lined about half the distance of both. These held mail sacks for sorting mail. The rear of the bus housed a small bathroom, which was removed within a year of entering service in 1941, plus storage for 150 sacks of mail. Other mail was sorted and distributed to towns along its 146-mile route in transit. It was powered by a 12-cylinder "pancake" engine that was mounted under the floor of the bus. The engine developed 210 hp. This bus consumed massive amounts of gasoline, averaging about four to six miles per gallon. The fuel tank had a 105-gallon capacity. This bus was officially retired from service in 1954. After its retirement, it was "hidden" by a well intentioned postal employee. To keep the aging vehicle from being declared surplus, the employee kept having it moved from one storage facility to another for years. The short stays meant that it would not appear on any General Services Administration surplus property lists. This kept it safe until the early 1960s when the GSA finally caught on. The bus was declared surplus and sold to a private collector. It was subsequently acquired by the Smithsonian Institution in 1968. This photograph was taken in front of the White House in 1941.

Although it may be hard to believe, this is the same bus that appears in the previous photograph. A steady progression of interior and exterior changes were made to this vehicle between 1941, when it was acquired, and 1960, when this photograph was taken. The gradual evolution in appearance reflects the fact that this particular bus served as the government's test vehicle. Because it was operated between Virginia and Washington, D.C., postal officials at Post Office headquarters could easily monitor the effectiveness of all sorts of modifications on this Highway Post Office before adopting them in similar vehicles nationwide. The Washington/Virginia route offered the perfect testing ground for a Highway Post Office. It had a variety of terrain conditions from flat to hilly in both rural and urban settings. Also, the mid-Atlantic region provided a full range of weather conditions in all four seasons.

One of the first three "Highway Post Offices" inaugurated in 1941 involved the experimental use of this modified International Harvester tractor-trailer. Used between South Bend, Peru, and Indianapolis, Indiana, the diesel-powered KD-8-F-COE tractor and the one-of-a-kind trailer quickly proved not to be a wise choice. It was plagued with persistent mechanical problems, it was difficult to maneuver into post office loading docks, it was prone to "jackknifing," and once on the road, the crew and driver were unable to communicate with one another. The poor showing of the nation's first, and only, tractor-trailer post office on wheels proved that this type of vehicle was not cut out for this kind of service.

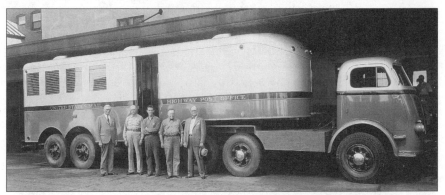

Reo produced this experimental Highway Post Office bus in 1949. Postal engineers were not impressed with its performance and few were subsequently acquired.

To improve traction in foul weather, many post-World War II Highway Post Office buses came equipped with "sanders." These devices, located in front of the rear wheels, dropped abrasives when the driver activated the system.

These three 1950 C.D. Beck and Co. Model 230 Highway Post Offices, photographed in front of the manufacturer's facility in Sidney, Ohio, were destined for use on two routes out of Des Moines, Iowa. Two of the coaches made one round trip a day, six days a week. The third was kept on-hand as a standby. The routes included Des Moines to Shenandoah (172 miles) and Des Moines to Muscatine (168 miles). The contractor that operated these buses was the Sedalia Marshall Boonville Stage Lines. The company was awarded a four year mail contract on March 11, 1950. According to the coachmaker's 1949 specifications booklet, "The Beck Highway Post Office has been designed to give the contract mail carrier a solid dependable practical unit at a minimum capital investment so that he may be in a position to realize a reasonable profit on his contract." The contract for the two Des Moines routes was worth $53,069.12. Power for the these Beck buses was furnished by an International Red Diamond 450 cubic-inch, six-cylinder engine. (Photograph courtesy of Greg Knuth)

By the 1950s, White Motor Co. was a leading producer of Highway Post Office buses, including these two variations of the same basic model shown leaving the company's Cleveland, Ohio, plant (top and bottom).

While the average highway post office vehicle offered distribution and storage facilities fairly comparable to a 30-foot-long railway mail car, the Twin Coach Co.'s "Super Twin" was 15 feet longer. First tested in 1949, this style of vehicle represented the largest bus-body built to that time. The test version was designated with an "X1000" identification number (top). The first "Super Twin" placed in service provided mail service between Washington, D.C., and Baltimore, Maryland (bottom). Although those cities are only 40 miles apart, the bus covered a circuitous 142-mile route, traveling east through Upper Marlboro and Annapolis, Maryland, before heading north towards Baltimore. Additional "Super Twins" were purchased in the 1950s, including this one that was between Los Angeles and Laguna Beach, California. The majority of these articulated postal vehicles were typically used between various Eastern cities.

Twin Coach Co. was a major producer of Highway Post Offices. Slight variations of its "Fageol" models, such as this 1951 version used in Ohio (top) and this later version used in Indiana in 1970 (bottom) were familiar sights on many highways.

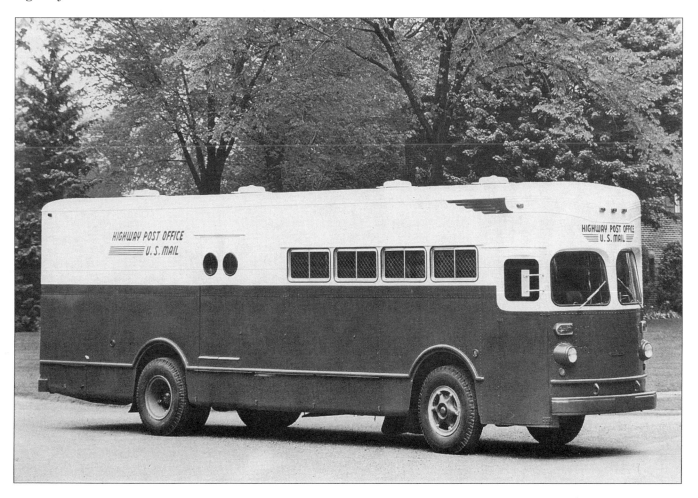

Powered by a rear-mounted Buick engine and weighing in at 28,000 pounds, this 1949 Flxible Coach Co. prototype Highway Post Office bus (top) was used between Williamsport and Altoona, Pennsylvania. A production model (bottom) entered service a short time later. The principal cosmetic differences between the prototype and the production model were in the curvature of the rear and the treatment of the windows. The prototype had three side windows and one large round door window on the side facing the photographer. Both versions could get up to about 50 miles per hour on level roads. As with other postal buses of this era, the exteriors were painted in a distinctive red, white, and blue color scheme. The interiors were painted white overhead, with green side walls. A major supplier of highway post office vehicles, Flx- ible Coach Co. supplied 13 Highway Post Office buses between 1949 and 1950. That represented about 13 percent of the new routes inaugurated during those two years. In 1952, Flxible, in cooperation with the Twin Coach Co. of Kent, Ohio, produced 38 additional postal buses. That same year, 27 new mail bus routes were inaugurated. In the 15 years follow- ing World War II, highway post office routes grew to include about 400 routes, many of which relied upon Flxible buses, but, by 1965, the ballooning growth rate burst. After that, bus routes were discontinued as quickly as possible. They fell victim to the postal system's growing reliance upon Mail Sectional Sorting Centers, large mail handling factories that were served by trucks.

Photographed in 1964, this 40-foot Crown Coach Corp. Highway Post Office bus was operated under contract to the Post Office Department by General Highway Services, Inc. of Dallas, Texas. At that time the Texas-based company was operating five of these postal buses.

One of two such vehicles used nationwide, this Highway Post Office was converted into a traveling museum in 1960 as part of the Post Office Department's "Parade of Postal Progress" program. This vehicle retraced the original route of the Pony Express from St. Joseph, Missouri, to Sacramento, California. (Photograph courtesy of the United States Postal Service)

A White Motor Co. Highway Post Office after being involved in a minor collision.

Even the biggest postal vehicles occasionally got hit, in this case a Raleigh, North Carolina-based Highway Post Office.

TRACTOR-TRAILERS

Trailer "V-17" was a 20-foot Dorsey DFC-S16 that was purchased in 1950 for $1,931.63. The trailer and this International Harvester CO series tractor (which was actually built by Diamond T for IHC) were used in New York City. (Photograph courtesy of Joseph H. Cohen, United States Postal Service, New York City)

In 1952, the Post Office Department acquired 100 tractors, including this International Harvester, and 300 trailers.

Late in 1953, the Post Office Department started "piggy-backing" mail aboard flat cars of the New Haven Shore Line between New York and Boston. This type of service simplified mail handling. It eliminated the need to load and unload sacks of Parcel Post and business mail onto and off of railway mail cars between destinations. This particular trailer is one of 32 35-foot Fruehauf Model 535s acquired in 1954 specifically for "piggyback" service.

In 1954, the Post Office Department purchased 60 White Motor Co. 3020 "cab-over-engine" style tractors, similar to the one pictured. Four years earlier the postal service purchased this 20-foot Dorsey DFC-S16 trailer. The trailer, bearing serial number "V25," was one of 90 acquired from Dorsey that year for $1,932 each.

In 1956, the Post Office Department purchased six Fruehauf 20-foot Model FD-CD522 trailers. These were assigned serial numbers 670001 to 670006. The purchase price for these 7,500-pound trailers was $3,600 each. (Photograph courtesy of the United States Postal Service)

Twenty-nine International Harvester CO-202 tractors were purchased for $6,074.82 each by the Post Office Department in 1959. This 175-hp tractor, photographed in front of the west front of the United States Capitol, is pulling a 35-foot 1959 COPCO Model T3593CSB trailer.

Vehicle maintenance has always been important to the Post Office Department. In this case, a postal mechanic is tuning a 1959 International CO-202 tractor. The trailer is one of 90 20-foot Highway brand SKD-3703s acquired in 1951.

This is the first of five 35-foot COPCO Model T3593CSB trailers purchased by the Post Office Department in 1959. These were the most expensive trailers acquired at that time. Each of the 10,380-pound trailers cost $7,000. The tractor is a 1961 GMC. (Photograph courtesy of the Library of Congress)

One of 40 1960 International Harvester CO-202 tractors, with one of 19 28-foot Dorsey DF-20 trailers, purchased in 1960. Each of the 99-inch wheelbase "cab-over-engine" International tractors acquired that year produced 175 hp. The Post Office Department purchased the tractors for $6,363 each. The price per trailer was $3,455.

This Mack MB-600 tractor was built under contract to the Post Office Department as a prototype at the company's Allentown plant. The prototype was delivered to the Post Office Department in March 1965. Production of additional MB-600 tractors commenced in April of that year.

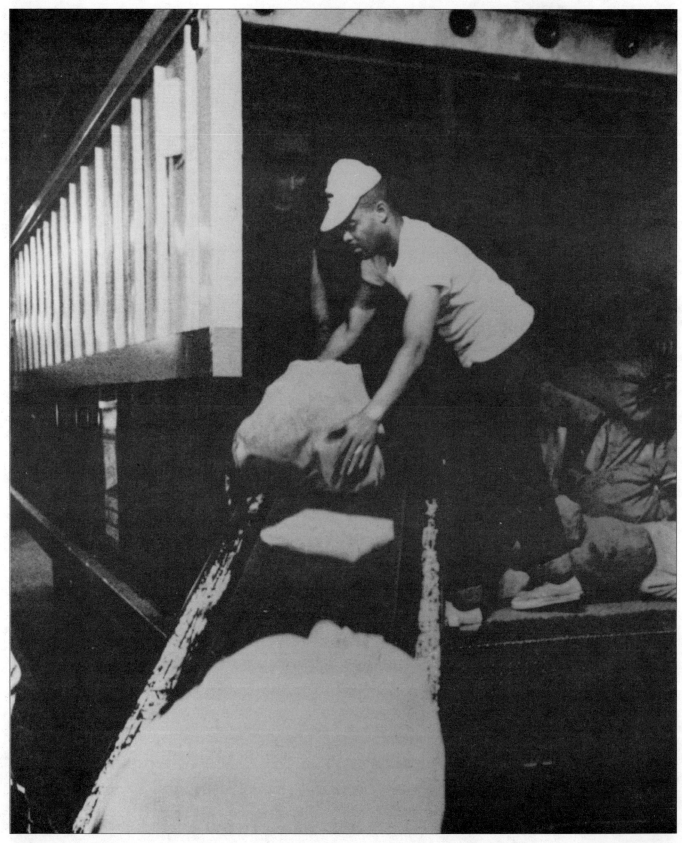

*Mail handlers are responsible for loading and unloading postal trailers. (Photograph courtesy of the United States Post-
al Service)*

This 28-foot trailer, manufactured by Fruehauf, in the mid-1960s was classified as an "experimental heavy-duty delivery semi-trailer van." Such vehicles were seen as a way of reducing maintenance and operational costs because of their rugged construction. (Photograph courtesy of the United States Postal Service)

Mobile post offices such as this have played a significant role after natural disasters. In this case, the post office was a 48-foot converted house trailer that was maintained in Detroit on standby in 1970. It was used in Crescent City, Illinois, after the local post office was destroyed by a fire caused by exploding tank cars of propane gas. This postal unit, one of 30 similar units stored at strategic locations around the country, was rushed to Crescent City with a state police escort, arriving while the fires were still burning. (Photograph courtesy of the United States Postal Service)

Photograph of the Chicago "Tractor-Trailer Control Board" in the central dispatch office in 1963. This board recorded the movements of up to 100 tractors and 300 trailers. Two-way radios enabled accurate communication between the drivers and the control room operators. (Photograph courtesy of the United States Postal Service)

A 1963 view of the Chicago truck terminal where the "Tractor-Trailer Control Board" was housed. (Photograph courtesy of the United States Postal Service)

A 1990 White / GMC tractor.

A 1996 Mack tractor.

A pair of trailers parked in the reserved slots for postal trailers at the Government Printing Office in Washington, D.C.

TWO- AND THREE-WHEELERS

U. S. MAIL
51

P-22384

USA
7
Chapter

At first glance, this "Indian" motorbike, manufactured by the Hendee Manufacturing Co., might be mistaken for an ice cream peddler's cart. Instead, it was used in 1908 in Washington, D.C., to test the feasibility of collecting mail on an urban mail route. This was basically a regular rickshaw-like passenger vehicle, then commonly referred to as a "tricar," except that the passenger's seat was replaced with a small package box. The box was capable of holding about 250 pounds of mail. Washington wasn't the ideal place to test such a vehicle. With its relatively flat terrain and wide paved streets, it was too easy a test site.

In the 1910s, Harley-Davidson manufactured an exceptionally versatile "Motorcycle Truck," such as these three that were used in the manufacturer's hometown for mail collections. These three-wheelers could transport up to 600 pounds of mail. (Photograph courtesy of the Milwaukee County Historical Society)

To expedite the collection of mail from curbside lamppost letter boxes, the Post Office tested using special drop-bottom mailboxes and special tricars in 20 of the nation's largest cities, including this one furnished by the Minneapolis Motor Co. To collect the mail, the tricar was stopped directly in front of the letter box and the driver opened the side of the tricar body facing the box. When the mailbox was unlocked the lower portion dropped open, emptying its contents directly into the body of the tricar. The 1911 trial was said to have reduced collection times by as much as 50 percent, but the idea of using both the three-wheelers and the drop-bottom letter boxes was subsequently dropped.

Christmas was the worst time of the year for a letter carrier, especially a rural carrier on a motorcycle. This carrier used a Harley-Davidson to transport the Christmas mail from Ottawa, Michigan, in 1915.

Two-wheelers enabled carriers to qualify for longer routes, which paid more money, and then to finish those routes in near record time, which further allowed carriers to get part-time jobs.

Motorcycles saved time and money. This rural letter carrier claimed that on a good day he could complete his 28-mile route in about three hours. The average cost per trip was calculated at 28 cents. He also did fairly well even in winter and on December 24, when holiday mail was at its worst. He observed that on December 24, 1915, "I rode my motorcycle and sidecar on my route in a six-inch snow on the level, and I did not run over two miles in high gear as the snow was too deep."

Considered to be something of a record, this rural carrier claimed to have delivered 57 packages weighing 247 pounds in 46 minutes, despite eight inches of snow.

Only a few years before this photograph was taken collections from curbside letter boxes in New York City and elsewhere would have been done on horseback, not with this six-hp Model V "Flying Merkel" motorcycle.

Mailsters to the rescue. In the event of a national emergency these 1957 Model 780-26 Cushman mailsters were to be used in New York City for civil defense. Many thought that this kind of planning was a farce. For one thing, almost everyone expected that New York City would be annihilated in a Soviet nuclear attack. And many postal employees claimed that mailsters were barely mobile on a good New York day, let alone capable of maneuvering over the rubble strewn landscape that would result from a nuclear attack. Despite such doubts, throughout the 1950s the Post Office Department participated in the Federal government's "Operation Alert," an annual nationwide simulated civil defense training exercise. Among the duties assigned to the postal system was radiological monitoring, emergency first aid, and the mass evacuation of able and injured Americans from America's major cities. Uninjured individuals were to be transported by any available mail truck, while postal tractor-trailers were fitted as ambulances that were capable of transporting several dozen injured at a time.

SERVICE
VEHICLES

USA

Chapter 8

Much the worse for wear, this battered Ford truck chassis supports a mechanic's truck body. Photographed in the mid-1920s, vehicles such as this were dispatched to make roadside repairs. In 1922, a single mail truck typically consumed 40 new spark plugs. On some mornings as many as one-third of the mail trucks in certain cities had to be coaxed into starting. As with most postal service tires at that time, those on this service truck bear the "U.S. Mail" brand. Branding was done to cut down on internal theft. (Photograph courtesy of the United States Postal Service)

This 1941-1945 Model G7100 Chevrolet one-and-one-half-ton tow truck was a welcome postwar military hand-me-down.

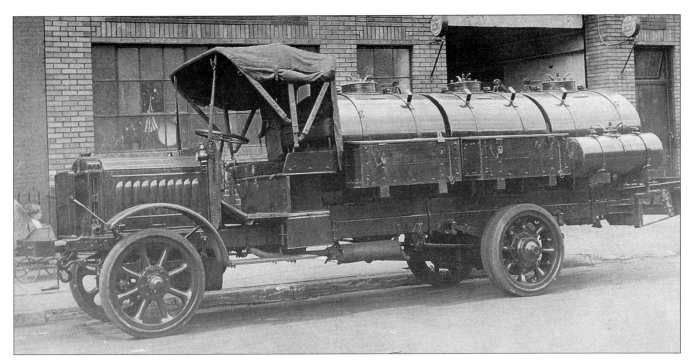

Riker trucks manufactured by Locomobile were often used as heavy-duty service vehicles during the World War I era. Most were three-ton (Model B) to four-ton (Model BB) trucks, such as this fuel tanker (top) and tow truck (bottom). (Photographs courtesy of the United States Postal Service)

This makeshift wrecker was created by cutting down the body of a Ford F-5 mail truck. The automotive face lift was carried out by postal mechanics at the Washington, D.C., vehicle maintenance facility in the mid-1950s. (Photograph courtesy of George Shifflet)

In 1959, the postal service purchased 100 Willys FC-170s primarily for transporting large amounts of mail from street letter boxes, although they also served as postal snowplows when necessary. The following year an additional 25 of these one-ton stake body vehicles were purchased for an average price of $3,198.96. These forward control transports were powered by a six-cylinder, 105-hp engine.

Buses, such as this 1981 International S-1200, are used to transport postal employees to training facilities and other large meetings.

This International bus, used for a variety of longer excursions, also was acquired in 1981.

The Postal Service has its own vehicle maintenance facilities in most major metropolitan areas, including this facility in Washington, D.C.

A Ford F-Series tow truck assigned to the Washington, D.C., Post Office.

Already old when it was acquired in 1965 as surplus from a naval air station south of Washington, D.C., this GMC "recovery truck" was considered one of the nation's capitol's finest service vehicles a quarter-century ago. (Photograph courtesy of George Shifflet)

The roof labels such as these used in New York City made it easy to spot a disabled or hijacked mail truck from the air.

This book includes only a few accident photographs. With a fleet as large as the Postal Service's, dramatic mishaps were commonplace—so much so that the subject easily warrants a book of its own. Every type of vehicle has been damaged in one way or another, from giant Highway Post Offices to tiny "mailsters." In the first half of this century the Post Office Department divided mishaps into two categories. Anything that resulted in $5 to $150 worth of damage was considered an "accident." Damage in excess of $150, such as was done to the Model A Ford pictured, was classified as a "wreck." In New York City, where there were never more than 170 mail trucks on the road at any one time, the collision rate was extremely high. On average, there were 36 accidents and three wrecks in New York each month in the 1930s.

SPECIAL VEHICLES AND EXPERIMENTALS

USA
9

Chapter

Horse-drawn omnibus-like wagons were used in several major cities as early as the 1880s to transport letter carriers to and from their routes. Within three decades such horse-drawn vehicles were replaced by motorized buses, including these three large buses built on Franklin Automobile Co. chassis, shown in front of the Washington, D.C., post office on November 15, 1911, the day service was inaugurated. The buses were furnished under contract to the Post Office Department with the local representative of the Syracuse, New York, car company. The contract was for four years. Each bus was powered by a four-cylinder, air-cooled engine. These vehicles were handsomely appointed with leather seats that could accommodate eight carriers inside the vehicle, plus space for one beside the driver and standing room for another carrier on the rear step. The rear portion of each vehicle also provided space for stowing the letter carrier's satchels. The vehicles were painted dark blue with "United States Mail" in gold lettering.

In 1916, the Post Office Department purchased 54 three-wheel Model 20 Wagenhal vans for use in conjunction with Parcel Post Service. Resembling a coffin on wheels, these chain-driven delivery vans were grossly overpowered, considering their 800-pound capacity. Priced at about $700 each, they featured a four-cylinder engine that developed 24 hp. The engine was installed crosswise over the single hard rubber rear tire. The driver's buggy-type seat was mounted over the engine. One of the Wagenhals was assigned to messenger service between the Washington, D.C., Post Office and postal service headquarters. Unfortunately, within a matter of days of its delivery a connecting rod broke. Despite the fact that new engine parts were quickly ordered, no one at the postal service was exactly sure how to make the repairs to the rear-wheel drive vehicle. The assignment was turned over to postal engineer Roy Joroleman. Aided by a mechanic, Joroleman completed the task in short order. To celebrate, Joroleman and his partner decided to take their repaired Wagenhal out for a test drive. In a journal of his accomplishments Joroleman recorded what happened next:

"Starters were unknowns. It had to be cranked by hand with a loose crank. At that we started the engine all right but the crank flew out, swung around and struck my mechanic in the mouth knocking out some of his teeth."

A few days later Joroleman and his toothless colleague tried again. By now a recent snowstorm had left the city's streets dusted and slick, so a tire chain was needed for the rear drive wheel. Because chains were stored in another part of town, Joroleman and the mechanic decided to drive over in the three-wheeler to get it. This was not one of Joroleman's better decisions. When the Wagenhal hit a slight incline at Ninth and E Streets the back end began to skid around. In seconds the rear wheel got caught in an icy streetcar track and the vehicle turned sideways like an out-of-control toboggan. The van smashed onto the sidewalk, demolished a trash can and came to a stop only inches from a crowded store front.

As an alternative to sending carriers to their routes on public street cars, these government-owned White trucks were used in Washington, D.C., to transport them to outlying routes in 1916. The truck on the right typically transported 20 carriers. The smaller trucks usually held between 10 and 12 carriers. According to the Post Office Department, such transports saved about $3,250 a year in street car fares and cut about nine minutes off of each carrier's travel time.

The introduction of Air Mail Service in 1918 created the need for more motor vehicles. The heavy-duty White truck was used for miscellaneous duties, such as transporting aircraft parts and maintenance equipment. The White automobile shuttled the pilots back and forth between boarding houses and hotels where they stayed between flights.

The postal service began containerizing mail shortly after World War I. This heavy-duty Riker truck served as the over-the-road mule for the containers, hauling them between postal facilities and Pier 72, North Shore, New York, for shipment by rail or ship.

Although only one "Philatelic Display Car" was produced, at one point postal officials envisioned producing a sizable fleet of this style of truck. Built from a 1931 White Motor Co. chassis with a furniture van body, this vehicle housed a display of postage stamps valued at $1 million. From 1939 to 1941, the truck crisscrossed the country, stopping at over 490 communities in an effort to stimulate interest in stamp collecting among the youth of the country. A Chicago firm was awarded the contract to modify the body, which was constructed for $6,500. By the time the exhibits were prepared and installed, and a few more coats of paint were applied to the exterior, the modifications reportedly cost about $30,000. On May 9, 1939, President Franklin Roosevelt and his first Postmaster General, James Farley, inspected

the newly completed truck on the grounds of the White House before it took to the road on its 20,750 mile odyssey. Its 2-1/2-year tour abruptly came to an end following the Japanese attack on Pearl Harbor. The truck was withdrawn from service on December 13, 1941, in an effort to conserve gasoline and tires. The truck was last seen rotting away on a postal service parking lot in San Francisco following the war.

These two experimental Willys Motors "Henry Js" were displayed in the central court of Post Office Department headquarters in Washington, D.C., in the 1950s. One was a "Corsair," while the other was a "Corsair Deluxe." Neither left-hand drive version was acceptable. (Photograph courtesy of the United States Postal Service)

This Nash Rambler right-hand drive station wagon was tested by the Post Office Department in 1954. It was basically a standard production line model. Unfortunately the independent front suspension failed several times during testing.

A great deal of automotive experimentation took place in the early 1950s. Before the Post Office Department finally settled in the mid-1950s on the mailster and the jeep as its standard vehicles for letter carriers, a wide assortment of handcrafted and commercially made mail carts and scooters were tested. Unlike the mailsters and jeeps that were to follow, this early experimental cart included a spare tire.

This 1954 experimental quarter-ton forward control panel small four-wheel vehicle was designed to compete with the three-wheel Cushman mailster, then under consideration as a vehicle for letter carriers. Manufacturers realized that with the tens of thousands of carriers nationwide, this might prove to be a major contract. Because it was not prone to flipping over, as three-wheel mailsters were, Reo Motors of Lansing, Michigan, hoped to land a sizable postal service order with this vehicle, but that did not happen. Instead, the Post Office Department elected to order three-wheelers. The body of this Reo was fiberglass. It was powered by a two-cylinder, air-cooled, 14-hp Wisconsin engine. The transmission was a three-speed manual unit with a magnetic clutch.

In the hopes of landing a major contract, Marco entered this three-quarter-ton forward control panel van in a postal service vehicle competition, conducted in Miami, Florida, in 1954. Although it had many novel features, such as front-wheel drive, frame-mounted differential, a centrally mounted steering column, and Dutch-style side doors with electrically operated garage-like folding upper sections, the Marco was not a star performer. Instead, the Post Office Department awarded a contract to Twin Coach for a much simpler three-quarter-ton vehicle that was also tested in Florida. Power for the Marco was provided by a four-cycle, 50-hp Hercules engine.

In 1954, the Post Office Department began repainting its vehicles. The change was from olive drab, with a cream strip (top), to red, white, and blue. That year, all new vehicles, such as this half-ton Willys L6-226 Jeep utility wagon (bottom), were to be furnished by the manufacturers in the new colors. The white top was said to decrease heat inside the vehicles, the blue lower portion reportedly reduced cleaning costs, and the red reflective strip was expected to increase visibility for other drivers, resulting in fewer accidents. This was one of the postal service's vehicle modernization and improvement initiatives introduced in 1954. It took about six years to repaint all of the nation's older mail vehicles.

These Jeep styles dropped by the wayside. Among the early attempts to use adapt Jeeps for mail service were these 1953 (top) and 1956 (bottom) right-hand drive Willys "Dispatchers." The 1953 version had a manual transmission. The 1956 style featured an automatic transmission. Both of these models had hinged side doors. In 1954, a sliding door version with automatic transmission was initially tested. That style became the standard.

This style of half-ton 4x4 was introduced in 1974 as a go-anywhere sport-utility vehicle. One of these Dodge AD100 Series "Ramcharger" trucks was shipped to Norman, Oklahoma, for testing in 1978. The trial was marginally successful, but not sufficient enough to warrant significant additional orders.

In the hopes of securing a multi-year contract to produce at least 99,150 "Long-Life Mail Vans" — an order that was estimated to be worth more than $1 billion — AM General Corp. submitted a test vehicle in a 1985 winner-take-all contest against two other competitors. AM General hoped to win the contest, thereby ensuring its domination as the principal provider of half-ton vehicles. During the previous decade it had built all of the one-quarter-ton jeep-like vehicles used for mail deliveries. This test vehicle failed to survive the grueling test course.

Mobile post office units, such as this, are ideal for stamp sales at convention sites, remote locations and philatelic gatherings. (Photograph courtesy of the United States Postal Service)

A Chevrolet postal police cruiser.

238

Officially called the "ComPac Van," but unofficially dubbed the "nose loader," this experimental five-ton vehicle furnished by Highway Products of Kent, Ohio, was envisioned as an alternative to the problems associated with backing a tractor-trailer rig into a loading platform. The notion was that it is easier to simply drive straight into a space and back the unarticulated truck straight out. If the vehicle could get within a foot of the loading dock, pallets could be winched directly between the loading dock and the vehicle's drop-down platform (at left). Or, if the pallets were on the ground, they could be hauled into the truck by way of a pair of trusses that could extend to that level (above). Although this type of truck was developed principally for the postal service, commercial orders were also expected.

A joint venture between General Automotive Corp. and Fruehauf operating under the name of "Poveco" was one of three companies that competed in 1985 to produce the Postal Service's new "Long-Life Vehicle." A Poveco vehicle was tested at the Uniroyal proving ground in Laredo, Texas. The three competing lightweight vehicles (one from Grumman Allied Industries and another from Ling Temco Vought/American General Division, plus this Poveco prototype) were driven almost around the clock over a grueling course that included sand, dust, dirt, gravel, 38,200 potholes, rain, snow, frequent stops, wheel-lock-to-wheel-locks, and occasionally a stray head of cattle to liven things up. After four months only the Grumman Allied Corp.'s vehicle was successful in completing the tests.

ELECTRICS AND ALTERNATIVE FUEL VEHICLES

U.S. MAIL

U.S. MAIL

According to Postal Service files, this Columbia Motor Car Co. electric was used in conjunction with the 1901 Pan American Exposition, held in Buffalo, New York. It was used to transport mail between the Exposition's temporary postal office and the city's main post office. This photograph was taken on July 29, 1901. The idea of using a motorized vehicle in connection with the Exposition was tested two years earlier. On July 2, 1899, John Lieb, the superintendent of Buffalo's City Delivery Service, and Truman Martin, the chief promoter in Buffalo of electric vehicles, used Martin's Columbia motor carriage as part of a 90-minute test drive during which mail was collected from 40 lamppost letter boxes. This 1899 test is believed to be the first experimental use of an electric automobile in conjunction with mail service in the United States. (Photograph courtesy of the United States Postal Service)

Although not American in origin, the proverb "There is no chance which does not return" seems to characterize a typical American expectation. It is a sentiment that irresistibly seems to compel us to give people (or their products) two, three, or maybe even more chances. On that score, the leaders of the nation's mail service between 1900 and 1980 deserve an "A" for giving battery-powered vehicles chance after chance after chance. Unfortunately, electric mail vehicles, such as this Waverly used in St. Louis in 1903, never had the "juice" to really make the most of the chances they were given.

The Washington, D.C., distributor for Rauch and Lang convinced the city's postmaster to try one of its new electric vans in 1912. The test vehicle was used briefly to collect mail from boxes and businesses. The trial was not considered an overwhelming success in large part because Rauch and Lang electrics weren't cheap. Prices ranged from $2,100 to $3,100 each.

Used in New York City in 1905 by a publishing house to transport printer material to the city post office, this Couple Gear electric truck was able to amble along over the five-mile round trip at about six miles per hour. The truck, which weighed four tons when empty, could accommodate four tons worth of cargo. It featured a massive Exide battery that furnished current to four electric motors, one for each wheel. The cost of operating the truck was calculated at one cent per ton-mile, a rate that the June 3, 1905, issue of Scientific American said "compares favorably with a gasoline truck, while there is not nearly so much wear and tear on the mechanism, or so many parts to get out of order."

Electric mail trucks were often the only postal vehicles that started in cold weather. Getting them going was one thing, but keeping them moving was often another matter. The smooth rubber tires on this Boston mail truck lacked traction, causing it to be abandoned during a winter storm. (Photograph courtesy of the United States Postal Service)

This 1,000-pound General Vehicle Co. panel body electric delivery van was produced in Long Island City, New York, about 1914. Early electric trucks such as this were popular with the Post Office Department. Postal officials accepted Thomas A. Edison's prophecy: "Vehicle transportation in cities and suburbs will ultimately be done by electric storage battery vehicles. There is no escape from the fact that an electric motor has but one moving part, and that rotates, whereas all other motors have hundreds of parts, mostly reciprocating."

Built to please a hometown crowd, this Argo electric, with its snub-nose Renault-style hood and 40-cell batteries, was capable of putting out a top speed of about 16 miles per hour. It was manufactured and used in Saginaw, Michigan. (Photograph courtesy of the United States Postal Service)

The Walker Vehicle Co. of Chicago, Illinois, was a respected manufacturer of electric vehicles during much of the first half of this century. The original photograph of this Walker electric mail truck was taken on April 28, 1916. The driver is Chicago postal employee Albert Pieper, Jr. (Photograph courtesy of the family of Albert Pieper, Jr.)

This quarter-ton Highway Products electric "HiCycle" mailster was extremely well constructed. Unlike most other mail-sters, which had fiberglass bodies, this version had a heavy-gauge aluminum exterior. Although 300 of these electric vehicles were acquired in 1961, postal service records indicate that most were subsequently "converted to gasoline." A steering bar was used instead of a standard steering wheel.

This experimental 1,500-pound capacity Cleveland Electric parcel van was only good for short runs. This one-of-a-kind prototype was literally developed from the ground up in 1959. Entering limited service as a test, equipment-wise it had an exceptionally fine heating unit for the driver's compartment, but not much else going for it. One of its unique features was that the driver stood ahead of the wheels in this right-hand drive compartment.

Introduced experimentally in 1962, this short wheelbase Cleveland Electric was highly maneuverable. It was field test-ed to determine reliability and operational costs during the early 1960s. These tests were not that impressive. Its heavy lead / acid batteries were reportedly built for Pullman railway cars. The batteries, which contributed much to its hefty 5,950-pound weight, tended to last only about two years. Another problem that frustrated postal mechanics was that the battery packs were wired in series, so that a break anywhere in the system caused a total loss of power. In addition, charging costs exceeded the price of gasoline, the power output never equaled that of a gasoline-powered vehicle, and replacement costs for the batteries exceeded the initial purchase price of the vehicle.

Between 1990 and 1995 over 3,200 Grumman Al-lied Industries with General Motors Truck and Bus Division "Long-Life Vehicles" were converted from gasoline to natural gas. These were assigned to 43 cities. According to the Postal Service, natural gas-powered vehicles afford a number of advantages over gasoline-powered mail trucks. The fuel cannot be siphoned, which makes the fuel almost theft proof; there is a five percent improvement in fuel economy; the engines last two to three times longer; tuneups are easier; and the fuel averages about one-third less than gasoline. The fuel tanks are made of one-half- to three-quarter-inch aluminum or steel.

Thirty leased Harbilt Electric Vehicle Co. "ElectroMail" vans were tested between 1971 and 1973 at Cupertino, California. The test involved eight- to 15-mile routes, each having between 100 and 300 stops. According to the Postal Service, during those three years the 30 vehicles were out of service for only eight hours. This trial proved so successful that in 1973 an additional 30 "ElectroMail" vans, manufactured in Manchester, England, were added to the Cupertino fleet.

The gasoline crisis of the 1970s spawned many experiments with alternative mail vehicles, including the use of various electrics, such as this Commuter Vehicle. Tested principally in Florida, the performance of this futuristic-styled vehicle was particularly embarrassing. (Photograph courtesy of the United States Postal Service)

Postal jeeps remained relatively reliable and simple to repair and maintain, except for a period when the American Motors General Corp.'s DJ-5E "Electruck" version (top) was tried in the late-1970s. The curb weight of the electric jeeps was nearly twice that of a comparable gasoline-powered version, thanks to the heft of the batteries. These electrics also were costly. The typical purchase price was about $5,700.

Outwardly identical to its gasoline-powered counterpart, this Grumman/General Motors Corp. "Long-Life Vehicle" is electric powered. It was converted along with 35 other LLVs from a gasoline-powered model in 1995. The 36 electrics were deployed in eight cities: Huntington, Harbor City, and San Francisco, California; Merrifield, Virginia; Phoenix, Arizona; Atlanta, Georgia; Boston, Massachusetts; and Harrisburg, Pennsylvania. The vehicles are powered by a low maintenance GM-Hughes AC-Drive system that is engineered to provide for service over a range of 40 to 50 miles on one charging. The Gates Genesis lead acid batteries are mounted beneath the vehicle with access to the GM induction charging system provided through a covered port above the right front wheelwell. The charging time averages between three to five hours.

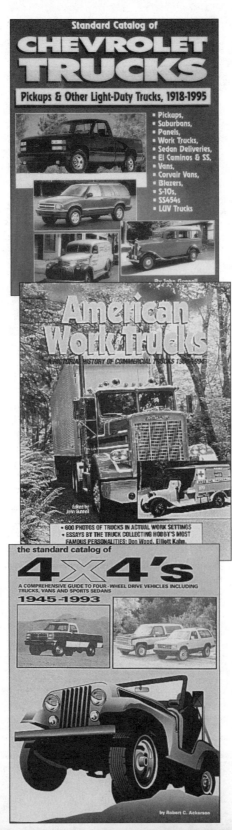